FEMINIST THEATRE

A Study in Persuasion

by
Elizabeth J. Natalle

The Scarecrow Press, Inc.
Metuchen, N.J., & London 1985

Library of Congress Cataloging in Publication Data

Natalle, Elizabeth J. (Elizabeth Jo), 1955–
   Feminist theatre.

   Bibliography: p.
   Includes index.
   1. Feminist theater--United States. 2. Theater--
United States--History--20th century. 3. American drama
--Women authors--History and criticism. I. Title.
PN2270.F45N37 1985   812'.54'099287   84-13965
ISBN 0-8108-1729-2

Dedicated with deepest respect to
Anna P. Scrivener,
who did not live to see my efforts through;
and with love to
Anna E. Natalle and Bernard E. Natalle,
who always encourage and allow
me to be an independent person.

CONTENTS

ACKNOWLEDGEMENTS

I wish to acknowledge the following people for their contributions while I was working on this project: Larry Hyjek, for constant moral support and encouragement; Kathleen Banner, Linda Noe, Mary Woods, Lou Ann Rimel, and Jon Natalle, for unquestioning belief in me and my ability to finish this research; Gregg Phifer, for superb editing and his demands on me to be more clear in my writing; John Degen, for his ability to always answer a question about theatre and for his constant corrections of my poor grammar; Wayne Minnick, for showing such sensitivity to feminist needs; Marilyn Young and Ed Wotring, for agreeing to help; Faye and Hollis Jackson, for putting up with me during the summer of 1982; all the feminist theatres and related people, for responding to my queries; B.M. and L.M., for their welcome senses of humor; and Rosa Rivers, for her expert typing and organizational skills which contributed to a final product that I am proud to claim. Thank you all for helping me reach my goal.

Theatre as Rhetoric

Since the inception of the modern women's movement
in America in the early 1960's, feminists have used a wide
variety of communication channels to transmit messages to
women across the nation. There are periodicals, antholo-
gies, television programs, films, and sound recordings--all
targeted toward women and all products of the women's movement. One medium of communication that has been largely
unexamined as a tool of the movement is theatre.

Over one hundred feminist theatre groups have emerged
in the United States since 1969.[1] Practically ignored by
commercial theatre, the feminist groups have provided a
means for creating and expressing a feminist ideology through
the dramatic form. Rhetoricians and theatre scholars alike
have overlooked the rhetorical and artistic importance of
these groups.

Of course, using the stage to advocate a point of view
is not anything new. Didactic elements can be traced back
to antiquity. Aristophanic comedy, for example, is laden
with political and social overtones. More recently, the plays
of Henrik Ibsen are often interpreted as reformist in nature,
and he is known for bringing serious social concerns to the
modern stage. In fact, A Doll's House (1879) was championed
by feminists of the time, although Ibsen disclaimed any intention of furthering the women's movement. Nevertheless, the
subject matter of plays like A Doll's House, Ghosts, and An
Enemy of the People shows that the stage could be used as a
forum in which to discuss social and political issues.

George Bernard Shaw followed Ibsen with his "Plays
Unpleasant." In these plays. Shaw demonstrated the negative
consequences of a society based on capitalism. His "victims"
faced alternatives such as slum landlordism and prostitution

as a means of economic survival. In his Preface to the
plays, Shaw said he intended "their dramatic power [to be]
used to force the spectator to face unpleasant facts. "2
     More contemporary figures, such as Erwin Piscator
and Bertold Brecht, have expressed political points of view
not so far removed from Shaw's socialistic outlook. Both
advocates of "epic theatre, " Piscator and Brecht believed
that the stage should serve to instruct the masses. Writing
about epic theatre, Brecht said:

> Right and wrong courses of action were shown.
> People were shown who knew what they were doing,
> and others who did not. The theatre became an
> affair for philosophers, but only for such philoso-
> phers as wished not just to explain the world but
> also to change it. 3

     In modern America, the plays of the Depression Era,
including those produced for the Federal Theatre Project
(1935-1939), have gained the attention of theatre scholars
and critics, who view the Living Newspaper plays in particular as powerful and effective social persuasion. 4 The prop-
aganda plays of the 1930's and 1940's and a large part of the
politically oriented experimental drama of the 1960's have
also shown the effective use of the stage for argumentation
purposes. 5
     Although it descended from the experimental theatre
of the 1960's, feminist theatre is one of the few radical theatre movements to be so deeply tied to a larger, specific
social movement.

Feminist Theatre as Rhetoric

     While there is some disagreement over which femin-
ist theatre was the first to be established, the New Feminist
Repertory and Experimental Ensemble, also known as the
New Feminist Theatre, was one of the earliest feminist theatres to emerge in 1969. The founder and director of the
now-defunct theatre, Anselma Dell'Olio, wrote about her theatre in Notes From the Second Year:

> For we are indeed setting a precedent--a first.

> This is one more reason for the word "new" in
> our name--there has never been a feminist theatre
> in all of Western culture--as well as the more ob-
> vious reason: the renaissance of the feminist move-
> ment. Our name also forms the acronym "free"--
> and that is easily explained as a desire to contrib-
> ute to the liberation of women from centuries of
> political, social, economic, and above all, <u>cultural</u>
> oppression. By this we mean not just "to give
> women a chance" in the arts, though necessarily,
> feminist theatre will be composed mostly of women,
> but primarily to give a dramatic voice to the new
> feminist movement. 6

Dell'Olio's words were important predictors of two
aspects of feminist theatre as it has developed in the last
fifteen years. First, she established the rhetorical intention
of her art, and in fact, feminist drama has become a form
of protest against the oppression experienced by all women.
Second, she acknowledged the idea that feminist theatres
would become places for women artists to develop their tal-
ents with other women, rather than in the traditional male-
dominated theatre.   While the development of women-run professional theatres is probably more of an artistic point than
a rhetorical point to consider, it may also say something
politically about the women involved in such enterprises.

For the rhetorician, an examination of theatres such
as Dell'Olio's is necessary in order to define the relationship between feminist theatre and the women's movement.
This examination is difficult for at least two reasons.   First,
the growth of feminist theatre has been erratic and unorgan-
ized. Groups of women, and sometimes men and women,
spontaneously came together in locales all over the United
States and at various times during the last fifteen years.
Many groups lasted only a short time, while others have
endured for more than ten years. This fact alone makes
it very difficult to establish any kind of homogeneity among
the groups.

Second, working style and political orientation vary
from theatre to theatre. Some, such as the Rhode Island
Feminist Theatre in Providence and At the Foot of the Mountain in Minneapolis, are collectives. Others, such as Joanne
Forman's Migrant Theatre in New Mexico, are basically one-
woman operations. Some theatres, such as the Orange County
Feminist Theatre in California, have male and female members.

Others, such as the Lavender Cellar Theatre in Minneapolis,
are lesbian. Trying to draw generalizable conclusions from
this diverse population is, again, not without a certain degree
of difficulty.

The Problem of Definition

        The fragmentation in form and style also makes it
difficult to define feminist theatre. At this time there is
not a genre called "feminist drama," nor do theatre critics
and historians acknowledge a specific type of drama that is
feminist. To compound the problem, there is the question
of how to categorize lesbian drama. While it has up to
this time been considered a part of the feminist theatre
movement, there are some who see it as a separate phenomenon.[7] Much of the dramatic literature produced by feminist theatres, including the lesbian groups, is still unpublished and, consequently, unfamiliar to theatre scholars.
        Articles and books on feminist theatre have devoted
considerable space to the problem of definition. Linda
Killian posed the question, "What is feminist theatre?" and
proceeded to say that it is many different things in terms of
style, ideology, and group structure. Her summation:

>   Generally, most will agree that feminist theatre is
>   theatre written by women which tries to explore
>   the female psyche, women's place in society and
>   women's potential.[8]

        Anselma Dell'Olio provides a more terse response to
the same question:

>   If, as has been said, the proper study of the stage
>   is man and the dilemma of his humanity, then per-
>   haps we can describe feminist theatre as the study
>   of woman and her sub-human status.[9]

        Dinah Leavitt devotes eleven pages in her study of
feminist theatre groups to the problem of definition. She
clearly rejects the notion that feminist theatre is "by, for
and about women." She regards this definition as entirely
too simplistic a way to dispose of the problem. Leavitt
demonstrates, through testimony from people active in feminist theatre and the arts, that variation in definition "is

very important to an understanding of each group's or individual's work."[10]   The definitions presented show a varying
concern for such concepts as "feminist," "political," "art,"
and the relationship among those concepts.

   While Leavitt is wary of placing a label on feminist
theatre, she offers a number of characteristics that pertain
to the phenomenon:

1. Feminist theatre and art are political and associated
    with the women's movement.

2. The emergent status of feminist theatre accounts
    for its variety in subject and its visionary point of
    view.

3. Feminist drama arrives at the universal through
    the personal.

4. Feminist theatre is pro-woman.

5. Feminist theatre is didactic.

6. Common characteristics of feminist theatre groups
    are collective organization, process orientation, a
    focus on woman's experience, community involve-
    ment, lack of money, and the use of experimental
    theatre techniques.[11]

   Leavitt's statement that feminist theatre is an emerging
phenomenon is important to the problem of definition. Feminist theatre groups have functioned only for the last fifteen
years and are still developing. Feminist art is in a state
of flux and critics are reluctant to outline criteria for eval-
uating feminist art, even though the development of a feminist aesthetic is a prominent concern at this time.[12]
   Since my own study is conducted from a rhetorical
point of view, perhaps some of the various artistic differences
can be minimized and a definition offered that is conditioned
by this rhetorical perspective. A rhetorician must view
feminist theatre as a communication process. The drama
is a persuasive message designed to influence the beliefs
and convictions of both the members of the audience and the
members of the theatre. The beliefs and convictions in
question regard women and their existence in a male society.
By using the stage as a speaking platform, feminists argue
against their own oppression, seeking a change in their
identity as lesser human beings and their subordinate position
in society.

This rhetorical perspective is clearly reflected in the intentions of this study, the first purpose of which is to determine the nature of the persuasive process in this form of communication. Second, the study will attempt to determine if the rhetoric of feminist theatre reflects the radical ideology of the women's movement.[13]

The first purpose involves an examination of the plays to discover feminist arguments and the strategies or proofs offered to support them. An attempt will also be made to judge the impact of the message on the theatre group members and on the audiences.

It is likely that feminist theatre involves theatre group members and the audience in a unique form of self-persuasion. The literature indicates that feminist theatre is strongly audience-oriented, that its activities often include workshops with community women during the writing of a play, audience participation during a performance, and audience-actor discussion afterward.[14]

While the emphasis of the first investigation is on the structure and presentation of the message, the second purpose is more context-oriented. By comparison it will be determined if the issues and arguments of feminist drama accurately reflect some of the major issues and arguments of the women's movement. This analysis will serve to place the didactic aims of the drama within a social context and to assess the potential impact of feminist theatre, as a communication channel, upon the women's movement.

The literature on feminist theatre is neither organized nor readily available. Articles and books are few in number and plays are difficult to obtain. Scholars have had to rely on a few cooperative groups in order to observe performances, interview group members, and gather background material. Because of the geographical distance between theatres, researchers are often limited by time and expense to a case-study framework. Dinah Leavitt's work with the Minneapolis theatres is a case in point, as is Janet Brown's chapter on feminist theatre groups.[15] At this time there is no clearinghouse for information specifically on feminist theatre, and those who do manage to obtain bits and pieces simply retain extensive personal files that rarely reach others interested in feminist theatre.

This research attempts to go beyond a case-study approach. An attempt was made to reach as many theatre groups as possible in order to assess the communication process. The evidence on which this book is based includes over twenty scripts, audience demographic data, responses to

questionnaires, personal interviews, observations of performances, and publicity materials provided by the theatre groups.
The data collected cover a wide range of groups and is
probably fairly representative of the feminist theatre phenomenon as it exists throughout the United States.
    Each chapter that follows focuses on a different as-
pect of feminist theatre as a communication process. In
Chapter Two, a general history is provided to acquaint the
reader with the development of the phenomenon. This is
followed by an exploration of feminist theatre as a multi-
locational rhetorical process, with particular emphasis on
the theatre groups as communicators.
    Chapters Three, Four and Five are an analysis of the
drama as a persuasive message. The chapters are divided
thematically, and each play is examined for the type of proofs
and strategies used in the construction of the message. The
analysis is based on Aristotle's rhetorical principles outlined
in the Rhetoric, including his categorization of discourse and
types of proof.
    Chapter Six is a defense of this author's theory that
feminist theatre functions as a belief-bolstering type of persuasion. Although the primary emphasis is on the audience
members and the effects of performance, the impact of the
theatre experience on theatre group members will also be
explored.
    Chapter Seven shifts the study to the second research
purpose, which involves comparison of the rhetoric of feminist theatre with the rhetoric of the women's movement. In
addition to setting up a context for the understanding of
theatre rhetoric, the chapter also assesses the viability of
feminist drama as a communication medium in the women's
movement.
    The final chapter presents conclusions and suggests
directions for further research in this area.

NOTES

1. For a list of American theatres see Helen Chinoy
    and Linda Jenkins, Women In American Theatre
    (New York: Crown, 1981), pp. 343-45.

2. Bernard Shaw, Plays Unpleasant (London: Penguin
    Books, 1946), p. 25.

3. Bertold Brecht, "Theatre for Pleasure or Theatre
    for Instruction," a selection from Brecht on Theatre,
    trans. John Willett (New York: Hill and Wang, 1964);
    reprinted in Dramatic Theory and Criticism, ed.
    Bernard F. Dukore (New York: Holt, Rinehart,
    and Winston, 1974), p. 851.

4. See Morgan Himelstein, Drama Was a Weapon:
    The Left-Wing Theatre in New York, 1929-1941
    (New Brunswick: Rutgers University Press, 1963);
    Caspar Nannes, Politics in the American Drama
    (Washington, D.C.: The Catholic University of
    America Press, 1960), pp. 102-20; Sam Smiley,
    The Drama of Attack: Didactic Plays of the Amer-
    ican Depression (Columbia: University of Missouri
    Press, 1972).

5. For an interesting discussion of antiwar plays of
    the 1930's-1940's see Caspar Nannes, Politics in
    the American Drama. Two helpful texts on the
    experimental theatre of the 1960's are Margaret
    Croyden, Lunatics, Lovers and Poets: The Con-
    temporary Experimental Theatre (New York: Mc-
    Graw-Hill, 1974) and Arthur Sainer, The Radical
    Theatre Notebook (New York: Avon Books, 1975).

6. Anselma Dell'Olio, "The Founding of the New Fem-
    inist Theatre," in Notes from the Second Year:
    Women's Liberation, Major Writings of the Radical
    Feminists, ed. Shulamith Firestone and Anne Koedt
    (New York: n.p., 1970), pp. 101-02.

7. For a treatment of definition and a discussion of
    the relationship between lesbian and feminist theatre,
    see Emily Sisley, "Notes on Lesbian Theatre," The
    Drama Review, 25 (March 1981), pp. 47-56.

8. Linda Killian, "Feminist Theatre," Feminist Art
    Journal, 3 (Spring 1974), p. 23.

9. Dell'Olio, op. cit. p. 101.

10. Dinah Leavitt, Feminist Theatre Groups (Jefferson,
    N.C.: McFarland and Co., 1980), p. 9.

11. This list is this author's own summary of Leavitt's
    discussion on pp. 16-17.

12. See, for example, Margaret Lamb, "Feminist
     Criticism," The Drama Review, 18 (September
     1974), pp. 46-50. Interestingly, Robin Morgan
     has addressed the aesthetic question in a satirical,
     but penetrating, one-act play that centers around
     a discussion by the nine (feminist) Muses. See
     "Art and Feminism: A One-Act Whimsical Amuse-
     ment on All That Matters," Chrysalis, No. 2
     (1977), pp. 69-87.

13. Patti Gillespie makes the point that feminist thea-
     tre advocates the radical causes of women's lib-
     eration. Her argument includes very little direct
     evidence from the drama. See "Feminist Theatre:
     A Rhetorical Phenomenon," The Quarterly Journal
     of Speech, 64 (1978), pp. 284-94.

14. For example, The Women's Experimental Theatre
     of New York conducts "public research" with women
     when developing a new play. This research is an
     integral part of the program that the directors
     have established. Charlotte Rea describes au-
     dience participation in the performances of It's All
     Right To Be Woman Theatre in "Women's Theatre
     Groups," The Drama Review, 16 (June 1972), pp.
     83-84.

15. Leavitt, op. cit. Janet Brown, "Plays by Feminist
     Theatre Groups," in her book Feminist Drama
     (Metuchen, N.J.: Scarecrow Press, 1979), pp.
     86-113.

Chapter Two
THE DEVELOPMENT OF FEMINIST THEATRE

The Emergence of Feminist Theatre

By the late 1960's the women's movement was a full-scale social phenomenon in the United States. Much of the initial force behind the movement came from women who had previously participated in the civil rights and New Left movements.[1] Unhappy with sexual double standards and the male power hierarchy, women activists began to turn toward the more immediate problems of their own oppression. Unaccustomed to having access to or control of mass media, feminists resorted to small-scale communication modes to explore the social, political, economic, and cultural ramifications of female inequality.

Brenda Hancock notes in her article, "Affirmation By Negation in the Women's Liberation Movement, " that public speaking by women to large audiences was not a common type of communication during the early years of the movement. The emphasis was on the small group, a mode of communicating that Hancock says avoided any kind of "hierarchical power relationships associated with masculine politics."[2] These small groups nurtured the development of consciousness-raising (CR), a communication strategy that is peculiar to the women's movement.[3]

Like women active in politics, women in the arts realized the difficulty of self-expression under male domination. The experimental or radical theatre was so caught up in the political and social turmoil of the times that it gave little opportunity for the women to dramatize the problems which were the focus of the burgeoning women's movement. Testimony from women who were active in experimental theatre shows that many of them recognized the fact that men controlled the theatre, a fact which forced those women to found their own theatres:

> The Mutation Show was the end of my work with
> the Open Theatre. I had to make a change that
> would articulate my being a woman. I realized

that the struggle for a woman in a sexist world
is so vast that wherever I worked the struggle
would be enormous. Until then I had somehow
thought that I was "equal" with the men in the
company even though I knew the outside world did
not think so. But when it came to struggles about
women, the men could no longer see the issues as
political; suddenly it was all very personal. [4]

> Roberta Sklar,
> co-director, playwright
> The Women's Experimental Theatre

It [the women's movement] enabled me to leave
New York and give up that whole careerism bus-
iness--the man's world of career stuff. I was
always acting as the woman behind a man anyway.
I was giving my energies to male careers. That's
what the women's movement freed me from, and
it also made me see really clearly that there's a
necessity to write about very strong women so
women can know that there have been strong women
in the past. [5]

> Megan Terry,
> playwright
> Omaha Magic Theatre

Anselma Dell'Olio's entry into feminist theatre began while she was working in a political cabaret,
the DMZ. She started taking feminist material to
the (male) director, who found it unsuitable at that
time for the DMZ. Dell'Olio, however, was con-
vinced that feminist theatre was a "dynamite idea."[6]

> Charlotte Rea, describing the founder
> of the New Feminist Theatre

This [The Mutation Show] was a feminist work,
and many of the women who worked on it have gone
on to create women's theatre. Tina Shepard worked
with Karen Malpede's group [The New Cycle Theater]
for a long time. Joanne Schmidman is one of the
people running The Magic Theatre out in Omaha,
which is a feminist theatre, and I have been doing
feminist theatre ever since. [7]

> Roberta Sklar, speaking about women
> in The Open Theatre

My experience with the Bread and Puppet Theatre
was stunning. It was fantastic. It was gorgeous.
It was beautiful. I also left them because I was
put on as a woman director and I was not given
the credit that I thought I deserved so I left
really for feminist concerns.

By the time I left Bread and Puppet Theatre,
I was disenchanted by their one, single-minded view
of women: which meant women should be barefoot
and pregnant and not be artistic leaders in the
theatre. Nor were the roles for women particularly
interesting, and I didn't like that. 8

> Martha Kearns,
> playwright
> The Wilma Theatre

By 1969 feminist theatres began to appear spontaneously in cities all over the United States. Thus another
channel of communication was employed by feminists who
wished to dramatize the issues of the women's movement.
In California, Bread and Roses Theatre functioned as part
of the Los Angeles Women's Liberation Union.9 The Orange
County Feminist Theatre was founded by Rosalie Gresser
Abrams, who was instrumental in founding the Orange County
Chapter of NOW (National Organization for Woman) two years
earlier. Since forming her own theatre group in 1971, Ms.
Abrams has used theatre as a vehicle for contributing finan-
cially to the feminist movement. All profits from the show
Myth America--How Far Have You Really Come? are donated
to the women's movement, including funds sent to women's
health centers, NOW chapters, centers for battered women,
and money set aside for individual women in need.10 In
New York, Anselma Dell'Olio's New Feminist Theatre put
on its first play as a benefit for Redstockings, and this was
followed by another benefit for the National Organization for
Women.11
    Other theatres that regularly performed at women's
centers and for feminist organizations include The Bread
and Roses Theatre and Synthaxis Theatre Company of California, Caravan Theatre and "Who's A Lady?" Company of
Massachusetts, Lavender Cellar Theatre of Minnesota, Onyx
Women's Theatre and Womanrite Theatre Ensemble of New
York, and the Washington Area Feminist Theatre of Washington, D.C.12 Interestingly, the Washington Area Feminist
Theatre (WAFT) was formed after some women had produced
two shows for the Washington, D.C., chapter of NOW in the
summer of 1972. During its four years of activity, WAFT

continued to involve as many women as possible and remained
close to the feminist community.[13]

The relationship between feminist theatre groups and
the women's movement is complex and ever-changing. Each
has affected the other over the years, and the interchange
continues as the women's movement itself grows and matures.
Feminist theatre is not only a voice that reflects the ideas
of the women's movement, but it is also part of the movement as a contributor of ideas. This dual function can be
seen more easily if feminist theatre is examined as a multi-
locational rhetorical process.

Feminist Theatre As a Multi-Locational Rhetorical Process

The concept of a multi-locational rhetorical process
becomes clear if it is examined in the form of a communication model. Consider a simple paradigm of human communication:

Fig. 1   Human communication (arrows indicate
direction of influence)

In a persuasion model the source attempts to influence the
receiver through some kind of message containing arguments
that represent the source's point of view. The success of
the persuasive attempt is measured by behavioral change or
verbal commitment from the receiver that comes back to the
source in the form of feedback.

In the case of feminist theatre, the persuasion that
takes place does not occur at just one point in the process.
Rather, persuasion occurs at many locations in the process.
Moreover, the persuasion is not always a source exerting
influence on a receiver. Both source and receiver engage
in self-persuasion as part of the total theatre experience.
Figure 2 illustrates the complex communication interchange
that takes place in the feminist theatre phenomenon.

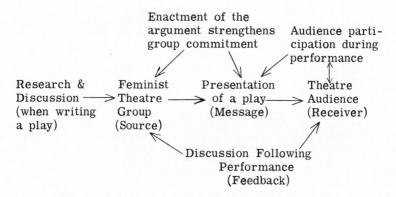

Fig. 2   Feminist theatre process (arrows
indicate direction of influence)

This model shows at least five locations in the communication process where persuasion is likely to take place.
First, the theatre group members bolster their own beliefs
on a feminist issue during the research and writing period
of a new play.   A new repertoire of arguments may also
be added at this time to support the arguments already known
to the group.

A second point is the message itself--in this case, a
play.   The theatre group attempts to influence the audience
by presenting arguments in a dramatic format.   If the play
is structured so that the audience is invited to participate
during the actual performance, then a third possibility for
persuasion occurs.   The audience is involved in a form of
self-persuasion by actively contributing to the corroboration
and/or construction of arguments pertaining to the issue.

It is also possible that the actual enactment (the physical acting out of a drama on the stage) of a drama serves
to influence the beliefs of the actors.   In the case of feminist theatre, the enactment serves to strengthen the convictions of the feminist actors.

A fifth location in the process occurs at the point
when audience and theatre group members engage in post-
performance discussion.   At this point the influence attempts
can go in either directoin.   Although the theatre group provides the discussion period as part of their presentation,
it is always possible that the audience may influence theatre
group members by providing new ideas.

Using the preceding model as a basis for discussion,
the remainder of the chapter examines the multi-locational
concept in more detail.   The last section of the chapter

considers the implications of this approach for the rhetorical
study of feminist theatre. Chapter Six will examine the persuasive effects that occur as a result of the multi-locational
process.

Feminist Theatre Groups and the Construction of Messages

        The process begins with women who are feminists and
who wish to create a theatrical experience from a feminist
perspective. (Some groups have included men, but most
groups are primarily composed of women.) In its early
stages, the first thing that many women realized was the
fact that feminist drama simply did not exist.[14] Drama,
for the most part, has been written by men, with women's
roles formulated from the male playwright's point of view.
Feminist theatre groups found this unacceptable and, subsequently, created drama from their own female experience.
To do this, the women in the group found it necessary to speak
out about their individual lives; thus a type of consciousness-
raising activity evolved. The women in the theatre groups
began participating in the same type of small-group communication experience that hundreds of other women in the
movement also experienced.
        Kathie Sarachild, who first coined the phrase "con-
sciousness-raising," describes the activity as a feminist strategy: "Consciousness-raising was seen as both a method
for arriving at the truth and as a means for action and organizing.'[15] The word "truth" is a touchstone for feminist
theatre groups. They are dedicated to conveying to their
audiences the true picture of what it is to be female, and
most groups consider this their most powerful persuasive
tool:

>   Basically, speaking the truth as we feel it is what
> we feel will persuade an audience the most.[16]

>   Sherilyn Brown,
>   The Rhode Island
>   Feminist Theatre

> To persuade an audience just present the facts.
> That's, in my opinion, all it takes. They overwhelm.[17]

>   Sharon Dailey
>   Indiana State University
>   Listener's Theatre

Women's experience and perception must be central.
We find situations that are true, that are good, and
that show a common experience.   Truth is a key
term.[18]

Susan Chast and
Sarah Ives,
Theatre of Light and Shadow

The "truth" that the members of feminist theatre
groups arrived at through their discussions provided the
basis for the plays they authored.   Thus, the creation of
feminist drama is the action and organizing step of the consciousness-raising activity.   The picture of reality presented
by the earliest feminist theatres included some aspects of
the female experience that had rarely been seen on a stage.
It's All Right To Be Woman, a theatre group in New York
City, presented audiences with short skits on such topics as
shaving one's legs (How I Lost My Hairy Legs) and bras
(Sags and Supports).
There was an intense preoccupation with the female
body and a woman's relationship to her body.   It's All Right
to Be Woman explicitly explored this relationship, breaking
down the conventional perspectives and taboos, showing
ultimately that being a woman is a positive experience.
Charlotte Rea describes the opening of a performance by the
group.   As the audience files in, the members of the theatre are singing and the audience voluntarily joins them.

The singing ends when one of the performers
stands up and begins touching her body; when she
touches her breasts, a kazoo sounds.   She can
touch her head or hands or arm but not her genitals.
She frowns, and the kazoo goes.   Her movements
finally become completely doll-like, mechanical.
Audience and performers sing: "our faces belong to
our bodies, our bodies belong to our lives."[19]

The theatrical experience generated by groups like
It's All Right To Be Woman was shocking, certainly, but at
the same time it opened up a range of themes that touched
upon every facet of female life.[20]   Over the last decade,
plays have been produced about sex-role stereotyping (The
Johnnie Show by the Rhode Island Feminist Theatre), abortion
(But What Have You Done For Me Lately? by Myrna Lamb),
pregnancy (Baggage by Deborah Fortson), motherhood (Tell
Me a Riddle, an adaptation of Tillie Olsen's short story, by
Bobbi Ausubel of Caravan Theater), rape (Abide in Darkness

by Delores Walker of Westbeth Collective), mothers and
daughters (Daughters by Roberta Sklar, Sondra Segal, and
Clare Coss of Womanrite Theatre), lesbianism (Cory by Pat
Suncircle of Lavender Cellar), domestic violence (Goona
Goona by Megan Terry of Omaha Magic Theatre), and historically important women (What Time of Night It Is by
Marjorie Defazio and Patricia Horan of Women's Interart
Theater).[21]
     Over the years feminist theatre groups have become
more sophisticated in their approach to playwriting. The
collective process is still evident, especially in groups like
the Rhode Island Feminist Theatre (RIFT), which prides
itself in its group playwriting skill. However, consciousness-raising has given way to a more elaborate research
period in which members of the theatre group gather information about the topic of the play. The research can
include reading books, interviews with people in the community, attitude surveys, and workshops with women's groups.
RIFT explains their procedure for the research period:

> The research period is set up pretty much by the
> director--what kinds of things we need to do and
> who will take part in it. The research usually
> includes some book reading. It also includes
> interviews with appropriate people. For instance,
> when we did Paper Weight, the play on women of-
> fice workers, we did a lot of interviews with women
> who worked in offices of various kinds and heard
> stories and so forth. With Internal Injury, which
> is a play on battered women, we went into shelters
> and talked to victims, as well as counselors, and
> things like that.[22]

     When Megan Terry began work with the Omaha Magic
Theatre on Babes in the Bighouse, a play about women in
prison, the theatre members went into the community to
conduct a survey on attitudes toward women criminals. The
survey form they used is actually included as an appendix
to the script. Similarly, Megan Terry and the Omaha Magic
Theatre joined with "academic humanists" to "explore how
language is affecting/has affected the status of women" in
preparing the play American King's English for Queens.[23]
The collaboration included seminars, interviews, and the
provision of articles and books by the scholars.
     The Women's Experimental Theatre (W. E. T.), in New
York City, has developed a program in which "public research with women on themes relevant to our experience" is

an integral part of the playwriting process.[24] Over a five-year period, W.E.T. spoke to "hundreds of women" as they were writing the plays in The Daughters Cycle trilogy. On the programs for Sister/Sister and Electra Speaks, the last two plays in the trilogy, W.E.T. thanks both individual women and such groups as Gay Women's Alternative. Lehman College Women's Center, The Glines, Hunter College, Jane Addams Center for Battered Women, and SUNY at Stonybrook.[25]

These three examples indicate the level of sophistication involved in the research conducted by the feminist theatre groups. The community groups participating in workshops with the theatre members are often associated with the women's movement. Thus, the research period provides a direct interchange of ideas between the theatres and active members of the women's movement.

During the research period, theatre group members gather evidence for the construction of arguments they will present in the play. Since the theatre members have voluntarily sought the information, this is actually a form of self-persuasion which results in a firmer commitment to the feminist beliefs already held by the group members. New knowledge in itself provides the theatre group members with evidence that may be drawn upon at a later time either in the playwriting process or during the discussions after performances. The possible effects of the research period on the theatre group members will be assessed in Chapter Six.

Audience Participation

Many of the earliest plays by feminist theatres were not full-length plays. Instead, several short skits comprised an evening's performance, much of the drama stemming from improvisations and audience participation. As Janet Brown has observed in her book, Feminist Drama: Definition and Critical Analysis, these skits were more rhetorically direct than some full-length plays, leaving the audience without any doubt as to the intent of the message.[26]

In feminist theatre, the audience is more than just a passive body viewing the action on stage. Ever since the first feminist performances, audience members have played an active role in the creation of a total theatre experience. The feminist theatres have a high degree of success with audience involvement, which is significant when one considers

the rhetorical effects of the phenomenon. After a performance
by one of the earliest feminist theatres, New York Times reviewer Rosalyn Regelson said, "The New Feminist Repertory
is really working at what other radical theatres pretend to
be doing--searching for a path in uncharted territory."[27]
The enthusiastic participation by audiences allowed both communicators and receivers to engage in a dialogue for the
purpose of exploring this "uncharted territory."

Examples of audience participation abound, and the
following illustrations are indicative of the experiences shared
by feminist theatres and their audiences.

Myrna Lamb has devised two endings for her popular
one-act play But What Have You Done For Me Lately?[28]
The play concerns a woman's right to have an abortion, but
the roles have been switched. It is the man who is pregnant
and who pleads with a woman doctor to grant the abortion.
In the original ending of the play, an all-female board of
appeals hears the man's case and votes to terminate the
pregnancy because he is a "potentially unfit mother." In
the other ending, the audience serves as the jury and decides the case.

It's All Right To Be Woman performed an improvisational piece known as a "dream play." The audience is
invited to relate their dreams to the actresses on stage, who
act them out as they are being told. This kind of exploration of the female psyche was very popular with the audience.
New York Times reviewer Georgia Dullea interviewed the
theatre group after a performance at Sarah Lawrence College, where the dreams of the students were enacted.
"Dreams, say the actresses, have no 'political' content.
And for that reason, they find that their largely female
audiences respond to them."[29] Charlotte Rea adds that It's
All Right To Be Woman acted out the dreams of women only,
causing frustration among some of the male audience members.
Founder Sue Perlgut justified their preference by telling Rea
that "the group understands women's dreams 'because we are
women; we don't understand men's dreams.'"[30]

At the Foot of the Mountain has created a ritual play
called The Story of a Mother.[31] The drama is composed of
a series of scenes and ceremonies that explore the complex
relationship between mothers and daughters. Audience members are asked to participate in the rituals by recounting
their own experiences. For example, in the excerpt printed
in Women In American Theatre, the first ritual is called
"The Calling Forth of the Mothers."[32] An actress asks the
audience to see the image of their own mothers. Then the
actress, as the Mother, invites the audience to respond to

the question "Are there things that you always said that you would like to say now?"

> The audience members, speaking as their mothers, call out "I always said" and finish it with a phrase appropriate to their own mothers. (Examples from production experience: I told you so; Now don't worry about money, money comes when you need it; If everyone else jumps off the bridge, are you going to, too?; You made your bed, now lie in it; Make your bed; But I'm not everybody else's mother; Wait till your father comes home; I hope you have three just like you; You'll never know how much I love you; This hurts me more than it hurts you; You know they're only after one thing.)[33]

In another At the Foot of the Mountain production, the audience is invited to give testimony about rape. The press release for Raped: A Woman's Look at Bertolt Brecht's "The Exception and The Rule" describes the purpose of encouraging audience participation:

> Audience members are invited to stop the play at any moment and give witness to their own rapes, both literal and metaphoric. These personal testimonies give the production an improvisational and uniquely communal dimension--a safe and ritualized space for women to share their own experience and to hear the experience of others.[34]

The testimony offered by the audience members is actually a form of evidence that is spontaneously incorporated into the message presented by At the Foot of the Mountain. One person's testimony serves as self-persuasion and as proof to other audience members.

Joanne Forman's political and educational puppet theatre, The Migrant Theatre (1966-?, now defunct), was entirely improvisational. Ms. Forman says she "seized whatever opportunities arose" to engage the audience in the political/educational process.

> When the female doctor came out to fix Punch's nose and fifty-five Belen, N.M. kindergartners said "You can't be a doctor, you're a girl" the puppets immediately engaged in a long discussion: 55 5 year olds left the show knowing that girls CAN be doctors.
>
> While performing an adult puppet show called

"Steam" wherein Punch is fired from the assembly
line, and takes it out on Judy, the audience and
puppets got into a long, long discussion about the
general situation of the working class, domestic
violence, jobs and daycare, etc. [35]

The preceding illustrations depict the range of situations in which audience members have contributed to a meaningful theatre experience. Together, actresses and audience
explore what it means to be female, and individuals participate in dynamic communication exchanges. The theatre event
may be a powerful rhetorical experience for each individual
present, for action is a more persuasive tool than passivity. [36]
Another location for persuasion occurs in the group
discussion that follows a feminist theatre performance. Although not all feminist theatres hold post-performance discussions, a great many do. Audiences are invited to stay
to discuss the play, feminist issues, and other related topics.
The structure of the discussion may differ from group to
group, but the intent is usually the same. Every person has
an opportunity to express an opinion, ask a question, or give
a reaction to the performance. The persuasion occurring in
a discussion may be two-way. The theatre group has the
opportunity to reinforce the message they just presented on
stage, while the audience members contribute additional
perspectives to the theatre group.
In addition to discussion, some feminist theatres
provide educational workshops. The workshops include sessions on theatre techniques and topics concerning women.
The Orange County Feminist Theatre offers a variety of
programs on such themes as sex-role conditioning, women's
health, language, dating, alienation, etc. [37] The Calliope
Feminist Theatre in Hartford, Connecticut, offers theatre
games in order to provide women with an understanding of
the creative process and to help them "develop their own
senses of creativity." [38] These workshops do not necessarily
follow a performance; in fact, a group like At the Foot of
the Mountain charges $400 for a two- to three-hour work-
shop and $200 for a lecture/discussion. [39]

Rhetorical Analysis of Feminist Theatre

The potential for rhetorical analysis is striking when
the communicative process involved in feminist theatre is

viewed from this multi-locational approach. Yet, only two
studies to date recognize that feminist theatre is rhetorical.
Patti Gillespie, in her important article "Feminist Theatre:
A Rhetorical Phenomenon," makes the assumption that "all
feminist theatres are rhetorical enterprises; their primary
aim is action, not art."[40] Gillespie's purpose is to provide
the reader with the reasons feminist theatres spontaneously
appeared. She attributes their formation to two basic reasons:
history and rhetorical need.

Historically, women in theatre had the experience of
both avant-garde theatre techniques and political participation
in New Left activities. When the women's movement appeared,
feminists drew upon their recent theatre experience, not only
for techniques, but also to meet the needs of what Gillespie
calls "the peculiar nature of the rhetorical problems facing
advocates of women's equality."[41] Briefly, the needs facing
women rhetors included: finding a communication channel that
would give a woman the self-confidence necessary for rhetorical success; finding a means to demonstrate the belief
that the personal is political; and finding a way to overcome
the paradox women experienced in which they simultaneously
proclaimed equality while asking social institutions to grant
equality to them.[42]

Gillespie contends that theatre provided the necessary
channel in which women could call for radical change in
spite of the aforementioned rhetorical problems. The symbolic and hypothetical aspects of theatre allow feminists to
confront without violence and to persuade without threat to
themselves. In this kind of situation, Gillespie says, "even
a timid woman may become bold enough to function actively
as persuader."[43]

While Gillespie establishes the rhetorical aims of
feminist theatre on socio-historical grounds, Janet Brown,
in her study of feminist drama, deals directly with the content of the drama to establish its rhetorical intent.[44] Using
a Burkean approach, Brown demonstrates what she calls
"the feminist impulse" in both full-length plays and the skits
and one-acts performed by five feminist theatre groups.
Brown defines feminist drama as "the expression of a woman's
struggle for autonomy against an oppressive, sexist society."[45]
The rhetorical motive, in a Burkean sense, must be this
struggle for autonomy.

The major portion of Brown's study explicates the
feminist impulse in five arbitrarily selected full-length plays.
These plays were all successful off-Broadway productions.
One is by male playwright David Rabe.[46] Brown recognizes,
however, the contributions of feminist theatre groups, and

devotes one chapter to an analysis of their work. About
fifteen short pieces and two full-length plays are examined
from the work of The Westbeth Collective of New York, The
B&O Theatre of Illinois, The Rhode Island Feminist Theatre
(RIFT), Circle of the Witch of Minneapolis, and the Boulder
Feminist Theatre. (Of these five companies, only RIFT is
still in existence.)

Brown states that the drama performed by feminist
theatres is based on "scripts written explicitly as feminist
rhetoric."[47] The Burkean methodology is not emphasized
in her analysis of drama by the feminist groups. Instead,
Brown shows how the feminist impulse is demonstrated through
four common strategies: sex role reversal, use of historical
figures as role models, satire of sex roles, and the direct
portrayal of women's oppression.[48]

Brown's study hints at the implications of feminist
theatre that are suggested in the multi-locational model discussed throughout this chapter. She mentions the fact that
group communication plays an important role in the creation
and presentation of the drama. She also recognizes that
the process of creating group-authored drama may have a
significant rhetorical impact on the group members:

> Thus, the experience of participation in feminist
> theatre can have a rhetorical impact on the group's
> members that is quite distinct from the impact of
> its performances on an audience. The scripted
> performances of feminist theatre groups may and
> often do lack rhetorical sophistication. But the
> process of creating the scripts might, nevertheless,
> have had a strong rhetorical impact on the group
> members.[49]

Brown's conclusion concerning the level of rhetorical
sophistication is drawn within the limitations of her methodology. The work of the feminist groups did not fit as neatly
into the Burkean scheme as drama written by individual playwrights. Furthermore, Brown's analysis of feminist theatre
is limited primarily to skits and one-acts. Many full-
length plays now available may show more rhetorical sophistication than Brown recognizes. Nevertheless, Brown's study
is important as one of the first attempts to show feminist
drama in a rhetorical framework.

This chapter has suggested that feminist theatre functions as a multi-locational rhetorical process. The next
three chapters will examine the drama itself to discover the
strategies and arguments used by feminist theatre groups to
persuade their audiences.

NOTES

1. See Sara Evans, Personal Politics: The Roots of Women's Liberation in the Civil Rights Movement and the New Left (New York: Alfred Knopf, 1979).

2. Brenda Hancock, "Affirmation by Negation in the Women's Liberation Movement," The Quarterly Journal of Speech, 58 (1972), p. 269.

3. Kathie Sarachild developed CR in the late 1960's. She outlines the steps in her article "A Program for Feminist 'Consciousness Raising,'" in Notes from the Second Year, ed. Shulamith Firestone and Anne Koedt (New York: n.p., 1970), pp. 78-80. Sarachild discusses the assumptions underlying the strategy in "Consciousness-Raising: A Radical Weapon," in Feminist Revolution, ed. Redstockings of the Women's Liberation Movement (New York: Random House, 1975), pp. 144-50.

4. Cornelia Brunner, "Roberta Sklar: Toward Creating a Women's Theatre," The Drama Review, 24 (June 1980), p. 33.

5. Dinah Leavitt, "Megan Terry," an interview in Women in American Theatre, ed. Helen Chinoy and Linda Jenkins (New York: Crown, 1981), p. 287

6. Charlotte Rea, "Women's Theatre Groups," The Drama Review, 16 (June 1972), p. 80.

7. Brunner, op.cit., p. 33.

8. Personal interview with Marty Kearns in Philadelphia, 1 March 1982.

9. Lillian Perinciolo, "Feminist Theatre: They're Playing in Peoria", Ms., October 1975, p. 101.

10. Rosalie Gresser Abrams, Letter to Jane Bosveld of Ms., 15 August 1980. Photocopy of letter received from Abrams, 4 October 1981.

11. Rea, op.cit., p. 81.

12. Many other feminist theatres also perform for women's organizations. The examples here are taken from two listings in Ms. magazine which specifically pointed out these theatres and their ties to the women's community. See "Ms. Gazette News," Ms., December 1977, pp. 89-90, and Perinciolo's listing, pp. 101-04.

13. Mary Wilkins and Cathleen Schurr, "The Washington Area Feminist Theatre," in Women in American Theatre, p. 293.

14. There are exceptions, of course, such as Alice Gerstenberg's Overtones (1913) and Sophie Treadwell's Machinal (1928). But, as Judith Barlow points out in the introduction to her anthology Plays by American Women: The Early Years (New York: Avon Books, 1981), "significant plays, comic or otherwise, were and are the exception rather than the rule." And Barlow is referring to significant plays by women. Quote from p. xiv.

15. Sarachild, op.cit. "Consciousness-Raising: A Radical Weapon," p. 147.

16. Taped response by Sherilyn Brown on behalf of the Rhode Island Feminist Theatre to interview questions, received September 1981.

17. Written response to author's general questionnaire received from Sharon Dailey, March 1982.

18. Personal interview with members of the Theatre of Light and Shadow in New Haven, CT, 1 April 1982.

19. Rea, op. cit. p. 83.

20. For instance, in Wendy Wasserstein's popular play Uncommon Women and Others, audiences find it amusing when there is mention of tasting one's menstrual blood (act I, scene viii) and when a character holds up a diaphragm (act I, scene vii). The acceptance of issues like these is possible in large part because the early groups dared to broach such intimate topics on stage. What was "radical" in 1970 is mild today.

21. Additional sources that describe themes in feminist drama include Rosemary Curb's "Catalog of Feminist Theatre--Parts 1 and 2," Chrysalis, No. 10 (1979), pp. 51-75. A general thematic treatment of drama by contemporary women is provided by Beverly Pevitts in "Feminist Thematic Trends in Plays Written by Women for the American Theatre: 1970-1979," diss. Southern Illinois University, 1981.

22. Taped response by Sherilyn Brown on behalf of the Rhode Island Feminist Theatre to interview questions, received September 1981.

23. Megan Terry, American King's English for Queens (Omaha: Omaha Magic Theatre Press, 1978), p.i. Babes in the Bighouse is also available from the Omaha Magic Theatre Press.

24. Statement of purpose received from Sondra Segal on behalf of the Women's Experimental Theatre, March 1982.

25. Programs received from Sondra Segal, March 1982. About 120 women are individually listed on the Sister/Sister program as contributors to the project, and even that is only a partial listing.

26. Janet Brown, Feminist Drama (Metuchen, N.J.: Scarecrow Press, 1979), p. 86.

27. Rosalyn Regelson, "Is Motherhood Holy? Not Any More," New York Times, 18 May 1969, Sec. 2, p. 5.

28. The play is in Lamb's collection of feminist drama The Mod Donna and Scyklon Z (New York: Pathfinder Press, 1971), pp. 143-166. The first performance was by the New Feminist Repertory in 1969, and the first time the audience served as the jury was at the New York Socialist Workers Party 1970 Campaign Kick-Off Rally.

29. Georgia Dullea, "Dreams Are What a Feminist Group's Plays Are Made Of," New York Times, 21 December 1972, p. 42.

30. Rea, op. cit. "Women For Women," The Drama
    Review, 18 (December 1974), p. 79.

31. For ATFM, a ritual is a ceremony that is spir-
    itually based and includes participation of actors
    and audience as a communal group. The cere-
    monies are derived from cultural aspects of
    daily life that lend themselves to a ceremonial
    format. Often there will be a repetition of action
    or phrasing by each participant, not unlike a
    religious ceremony. ATFM is continually ex-
    perimenting with the use of ritual as a struc-
    tural aspect of drama, and, as such, is difficult
    to define. This description was provided by
    Martha Boesing in a telephone interview, 5
    September 1982.

32. Martha Boesing, "The Story of a Mother, a
    Ritual Drama," in Women In American Theatre,
    pp. 44-50. The Calling Forth of the Mothers,
    pp. 45-46.

33. Ibid., p. 45. Audience responses recorded and
    transcribed by Ellen Anthony.

34. Press release received from At the Foot of the
    Mountain, September 1981. Raped was first
    performed in Minneapolis, 27 June 1980.

35. Letter received from Joanne Forman, 28 Jan-
    uary 1982.

36. Active participation in a belief-bolstering per-
    suasive situation has been investigated by
    William J. McGuire. His findings indicate
    that public commitment to a belief enhances
    the strength of that belief, and that active par-
    ticipation in the creation of belief-bolstering
    messages has longer-lasting effects than pas-
    sive reception of a supportive message. See
    "Resistance to Persuasion Conferred by Active
    and Passive Prior Refutation of the Same and
    Alternative Counter arguments," Journal of Ab-
    normal and Social Psychology, 63 (1961), pp.
    326-332, and "The Nature of Attitudes and Attitude
    Change," in The Handbook of Social Psychology,
    ed. G. Lindzey and E. Aronson (Reading, MA:
    Addison-Wesley, 1969), pp. 136-314.

37. Flyer received from the Orange County Feminist Theatre, October 1981.

38. Written response to author's general questionnaire received from Sharon Wood, December 1981.

39. Flyer received from At the Foot of the Mountain, September 1981. Martha Boesing has noted that these prices are negotiable. A sliding scale is often used when a host group wants a workshop but cannot afford to pay the full price. Most often only universities can pay the entire fee. Telephone interview, 5 September 1982.

40. Patti Gillespie, "Feminist Theatre: A Rhetorical Phenomenon," The Quarterly Journal of Speech, 64 (1978), p. 286.

41. Ibid., p. 287.

42. Ibid., pp. 287-88.

43. Ibid., p. 289.

44. Brown, op. cit. pp. 86-113.

45. Ibid., p. 1.

46. The plays analyzed in the study are The Bed Was Full by Rosalyn Drexler, In the Boom Boom Room by David Rabe, Wine in the Wilderness by Alice Childress, Birth and After Birth by Tina Howe, and for colored girls who have considered suicide/ when the rainbow is enuf by Ntozake Shange.

47. Brown, op. cit., p. 86.

48. Ibid., pp. 88-108.

49. Ibid., p. 145.

The model described in the previous chapter indicates
that the drama authored by feminist theatre groups is message-
oriented. Indeed, the emphasis in these plays is on moral
instruction of an audience, even though many feminist groups
deny sacrificing the artistic aims of the drama in favor of
rhetorical strategies. The drama functions as the key element in the communicative process, for it is within the drama
that we find the feminist ideas which are of the greatest concern to the theatre groups.

In the following three chapters, the didactic aims of
feminist theatre groups will be explored through an analysis
of twenty plays that have been performed by ten different
feminist theatres. The plays date from 1967 to 1982 and
cover a broad range of topics and styles.

The most important criterion for selection was that
the play had to have been written and/or performed by members of a feminist theatre group. A second criterion was
that the play had to be a full-length drama. This require-
ment seemed necessary in order to go beyond the focus of
previous studies. However, three well-known one-act plays
are included for their historical value. They are The Independent Female by Joan Holden, But What Have You Done
For Me Lately? by Myrna Lamb, and Love Song for an
Amazon by Martha Boesing.

Each chapter is categorized according to the central
idea that permeates the group of plays selected for analysis.
Although a single play may address more than one feminist
issue, the category in which it is placed identifies the main
tendency of the drama. In this chapter there are eight plays
under the heading "sexual politics." Chapter Four analyzes
six plays in a category entitled "the woman-identified woman, "
and Chapter Five follows with six more plays in a category
called "family roles and relationships."

Within each category individual plays will be examined
for the types of proof, or persuasive strategies, that feminist
theatre groups have employed to argue their case to an audience. Aristotle tells us in the Poetics that the six parts of

tragedy are plot, character, thought, diction, music, and
spectacle.[1] The element of thought is crucial in the consideration of didactic drama, for it is the playwright's thought
that is being conveyed to the audience above all else. Aristotle says:

> Concerning Thought, we may assume what is said
> in the Rhetoric, to which inquiry the subject more
> strictly belongs. Under Thought is included every
> effect which has to be produced by speech, the
> subdivisions being--proof and refutation, the excita-
> tion of the feelings, such as pity, fear, anger, and
> the like, the suggestion of importance or its oppo-
> site.[2]

At Aristotle's suggestion, it seems appropriate to turn to the
Rhetoric as a basis for examining drama as a persuasive
message.

Recent research by Sam Smiley shows that an Aristotelian method can be successfully used in the analysis of
didactic plays. Using a sample of forty-one plays from the
Depression Era, Smiley discovered the presence of both
rhetorical and poetic principles in the structure of the plays.
The Aristotelian criteria used in Smiley's study included the
three modes of proof, the three kinds of rhetoric, and the
method of rhetorical disposition.[3] In an article preliminary
to the study of Depression-period plays, Smiley showed how
the same principles could be applied to a wide variety of
didactic drama, using examples ranging from ancient Greek
plays to contemporary plays.[4]

When defining the purpose of a didactic playwright
Smiley said:

> The primary concern of the didactic dramatist is
> with the thoughts that may be clearly conveyed to,
> or implanted in, an audience. Like an orator, a
> didactic dramatist is concerned with acting upon au-
> diences in ways that will result in conviction and
> perhaps in overt action on their part.[5]

The feminist theatre groups function as didactic dramatists in
the way Smiley describes in the passage above. The convic-
tion-forming aspect is especially important, for feminist
drama appears to intensify beliefs that already exist in the
mind of the primarily female audience.[6] The proof offered
in the words and actions of the characters onstage helps
audience members (and theatre group members) anchor their
convictions about feminist ideas.

What are the rhetorical approaches that can be dis-
cerned in a message? Three types of discourse are outlined
in Aristotle's Rhetoric.[7] First there is the deliberative
speech, which is essentially a speech to advise others on a
particular course of action. The speaker either exhorts or
dissuades the audience in regard to the matter, and the
advice is generally about future events and actions. A good
example of deliberative address is argument conducted in the
legislative chamber, for example, an argument in favor of
the Equal Rights Amendment. The second kind of discourse
is forensic, and the purpose is to accuse or defend the actions of someone; actions that have already taken place.
This kind of speaking is what we know as legal argument and
is most common in the courtroom. The third type of speech
is known as epideictic, in which the speaker praises or
blames someone or something. The speaker is most concerned with desirable or undesirable qualities and conditions
in relation to the person or object being spoken about. An
address commemorating the contributions of Susan B. Anthony
to the women's movement would be an example of epideictic
speaking.

Common to all three types of discourse are the proofs
used in the construction of the message. Aristotle defines
three kinds of proof, or means of persuasion: logical argument, emotional argument, and the credibility of the speaker
as a means of inducing belief.[8] While Aristotle points out
that the emphasis on the type of proof used may differ according to the kind of discourse, all three modes of proof
are available to the speaker when constructing a message.
It will become apparent in the forthcoming analysis that
different feminist groups confront the issue of sexual politics using all three forms of proof and all three types of
discourse.

This chapter takes its name from Kate Millett's
well-known theory of sexual politics. Millett describes politics as "power-structured relationships, arrangements
whereby one group of persons is controlled by another."[9]
The two groups in this theory are men and women, and the
power exerted is in the form of sexual domination. Millett
asserts that the institutionalization of male domination is
"perhaps the most pervasive ideology of our culture and
provides its most fundamental concept of power."[10] It is
this preoccupation with the power of patriarchy that provides
the common thread among the eight plays in this group.
Although the rhetorical approach differs among the plays,
all of them depict the concept of male power in society and
the resulting consequences for women. The playwrights

are arguing in favor of rejecting the status quo, even though
an alternative is not always suggested.

Myrna Lamb's one-act play, But What Have You Done
For Me Lately?, is an excellent example of drama structured
as forensic argument.[11] The issue on which the play focuses
is the right to have an abortion, but Lamb has reversed the
roles of the pregnant person and the doctor/psychiatrist. The
doctor is a woman and her "patient" is a man who has become pregnant by means of an implanted impregnated uterus.
Throughout the play the woman and man argue over the man's
right to control his own body and to be granted an abortion.
The irony of the situation is that this man and woman had
an affair years before while attending the same university,
an affair which resulted in an unwanted pregnancy for her.
Because of the patriarchal social system, the woman was
forced to interrupt her life to bear a child, while the man
pursued his law studies. The woman recalls with bitterness:

> Our individual unique familiar bodies, suddenly
> invaded by strange unwelcome parasites, and we
> were denied the right to rid our own bodies of
> these invaders by a society dominated by righteous
> male chauvinists of both sexes who identified with
> the little clumps of cells and gave them precedence
> over the former owners of the host bodies. (p. 158)

The woman is actually advancing an accusation against this
man, who represents all men, of using patriarchal dominance to the detriment of all women. Not only is this man
guilty of impregnating the woman in the past, but his crime
is exacerbated by the fact that he is a lawmaker and continues to support legislation that leaves women without control
over their personal lives.

Now that the man is pregnant, he suddenly defends
his right to control his own body with the same arguments
that women use, but males do not heed. By using the role
reversal of characters, the playwright is able to use a
rational mode of proof in which the utterances made by an
opponent (men) against a speaker (women) are turned against
that opponent.[12] When a woman is pregnant and wishes to
have an abortion, there are several arguments she will use
when asking a doctor to perform the abortion. These arguments include a description of psychic stress caused by the
pregnancy, the argument that a fetus is not a human being
and therefore has no rights, the argument that the mother
is sacrificing a career in order to bear an unwanted child,
the argument that an "accidental" pregnancy costs a woman

so much humiliation that she is rejected by friends and family, and the argument that birth may cause physical harm to the mother. In the play, the pregnant man uses all of these arguments to try to convince the woman doctor that she should grant him an abortion. The doctor refutes him by telling him he is "confused" and says those arguments, when used by a woman, are often dismissed by doctors. Since this man represents all men, the female doctor turns the typical patriarchal reaction against him and refuses to perform the abortion.

While the male character in the play is pleading for justice in what he deems to be an unjust situation, the female doctor continues to accuse him (and by extension, the partiarchy) of universal injustice to women who are in the same situation as this man:

> The dogma of beneficial motherhood has been handed down by men. If a woman spews out children, she will be sufficiently exhausted by the process never to attempt art, music, literature or politics.... That [having children] will occupy her sufficiently to keep her from competing successfully with male human beings on any other human basis. (p. 154)

The "dogma of beneficial motherhood" is not only male created, but is also enforced by male social institutions such as the church and the medical profession (p. 152).

Finally the doctor launches into an emotional argument describing the tremendous guilt and humiliation that a woman suffers from a pregnancy that is considered by society to be criminal. She points out that not only is the male partner deemed not guilty of any crime, but also receives no punishment (p. 160). The woman doctor is angry and is used by the playwright to arouse the anger of the audience members at the injustice of the patriarchal system. At the same time a certain amount of fear is aroused as the consequences of unwanted pregnancy are described. The audience is shown that effects are physical, psychological, and emotional, and that they determine not only the quality of one's life, but also the future relationships a woman can expect with family, friends, and possible lovers.

The pregnant man eventually admits his guilt, not only of committing a crime as a result of the affair with this woman, but as a lawmaker who supported strict abortion laws, thereby destroying the personal lives of thousands of women. The man then begs the doctor to appeal his sentence. She submits his plea to the all-woman board of appeals as

he promises to undo the harm he has caused by introducing
new legislation. The board votes to terminate the pregnancy
out of "compassion for the potential child" and the recognition of the man as a "potentially unfit mother" (p. 166).
Aristotle says the ends of forensic argument are justice and injustice.[13] In this play, Lamb has the woman doctor
argue against the injustice of the code of sexual politics. The
right to decide upon a course of action for one's own body is
the "highest representation of knowledge that one is master
of one's fate" (p. 164), but the injustice goes beyond the lack
of control of one's body. As the woman pointed out in her
earlier speech, the acceptance and perpetuation of patriarchy
precludes women from participating in many areas of social
and cultural life. The anger expressed by the woman doctor
is representative of the anger felt by all women who have
experienced a similar situation. The audience is shown what
it's like to be in that position--women identify with the doctor,
while men identify with the impregnated man who is forced
to see the issue from the woman's point of view.
        Even though the play is structured internally as fo-
rensic argument, it should be noted that the overall impact
of the play is derived from the deliberative ends of the drama.
Myrna Lamb is urging the audience to reject patriarchy and
its code of sexual politics. The abortion question, which
serves as the focus for discussion in the play, is simply a
vehicle used by the playwright to offer the audience advice
about the real cause of every woman's plight. However, an
alternative to the patriarchal system is not offered at the end
of the play. There is no solution, only the naming of the
enemy. This is a logical conclusion for the play, considering
that it was written in 1969. This was an angry time for
feminists and "naming the enemy" was one of the first kinds
of rhetoric to emerge from the women's movement.[14]
        The Johnnie Show, written and performed by the Rhode
Island Feminist Theatre (RIFT) in 1974, is also a role-
reversal play.[15] The drama is a satire paralleling The Tonight Show, but Johnny Carson and Ed McMahon have been
replaced by two women hosts named Johnnie Carlton and Edie
McMann. The guests on the show include Fred Walker (an
athlete from the Gentlemen's Olympics), Caesar Schlamonz
(an actor and ex-pinup boy), Mark Hastings (winner of the
Mr. California contest), and Dr. June Elliot (a doctor of
male sexuality). Johnnie and Edie are portrayed as sexists
who flirt with and cajole their guests (except Dr. Elliot),
just as a talk-show host condescends to a woman guest in
real life.

Intercut with the segments of The Johnnie Show (which include commercials by Edie McMann!) are scenes from Mark Hastings' home life. Again, the roles are reversed. Mark's father is the homemaker and his mother is the breadwinner in the family. In the home scenes, the audience finds out that Mark is a member of the "Maleist Movement." He won the Mr. California contest as a political strategy to expose the humiliation and dehumanization of beauty contests.

When Mark makes his appearance on The Johnnie Show, both Johnnie and Dr. Elliot try to disgrace him by not taking him seriously. They tell him that he is "confused" about his identity and refuse to talk about "Male Lib." When Mark insists that he would like "to talk more about the Maleist Movement," Johnnie asks, "Well, are you sure you have your parents' permission?" (p. 66). This is followed by Caesar Schlamonz's comment:

> You know, I can remember the days when I had to
> worry all the time about what my parents would let
> me do or say in public. It was really a problem,
> you know, because parents always want their little
> boy to be a charming young gentleman and say only
> the polite thing all the time. (chuckling) When
> I was little, sometimes I even wished I was a girl,
> just so I could say whatever I wanted to say. (p. 66)

After a few more barbs like this, Mark Hastings is utterly frustrated. Johnnie says there isn't any more time left in the show, and the play ends with Johnnie thanking her guests and wishing the audience goodnight.

Although RIFT does not offer a solution to the role problem exposed in the play, the audience is given the opportunity to "stop and think" about the whole system of sexual politics and the effects it has on the subordinate group. The role reversal of characters is used as a rhetorical strategy in the same way that Myrna Lamb employed the reversal in But What Have You Done For Me Lately? The men in the audience are seeing the typical male words and actions used against the male characters in the play. Johnnie, Edie, and Mark's mother use (real-life) male superiority to keep all the men under control. The men in the play are all characterized by female traits, and they demonstrate a kind of forced empathy with the plight of women in real life. By letting the male audience members see what life is like from a woman's perspective, the men in the audience should come to the realization that their dominance over women is wrong.

The satirical take-off on The Tonight Show is a demonstration of the ways in which television is used as a tool
to socialize people into stereotypical roles. The four commercials done by Edie McMann are especially effective. The
first one is for "Single-Boy Creme Rinse--for the boy with
a night life!" (p. 5). The last one urges viewers to buy
Dutch Girl Paints. Edie narrates:

> One lonely night you tried to brighten up your
> bedroom wall. Your wife came home from the
> office and was not too pleased with your attempts
> at creativity. But all is not lost. She covered
> it with Dutch Girl Paint. Wow, it sure goes on
> easy. You had to ask, "Isn't there anything you
> can't do?" And she said, "My husband. I think
> I'll keep him." (p. 56)

Not only do the commercials point out how ridiculous the
advertisements can be, but they expose the sexist nature of
the advertising techniques. RIFT is showing how advertising
itself is a patriarchal institution that functions as a control
over women's lives. After all, women are the primary
target of much television advertising, and sexual appeals are
one way advertisers have consistently sold products to women.
       The role reversal in both the preceding plays serves
as an effective rhetorical strategy. The playwrights use the
reversal to pose the question to male audience members,
"How would you feel if you were in a woman's position in
which your life was controlled by men and their code of
sexual domination?" We know what the expected response
is. The women in the audience should feel reinforced about
their own feelings of subordination in a patriarchal society.
Even though neither play tells women what to do to gain
equality of control, they can be sure that the first action to
take is resistance to male domination.
       In the next two plays, the injustice of sexual politics
is demonstrated using rape as a point of illustration. Both
plays are deliberative discourse, and both advise the audience
to reject male power politics in favor of a society that is
characterized by either androgynous or matriarchal traits.
       Persephones [sic] Return, written by the Rhode Island
Feminist Theatre (RIFT) and first performed in 1974, is
based upon the myth of Demeter and Persephone.[16] Intercut
with mythological scenes are scenes from the lives of modern
couples. In the introduction to the play, RIFT explains:

The mother/daughter bond, severed by the powers
of the patriarchy (men), seemed universal and personal to us all. The myth is the main theme of
the play, one that we continually returned to as we
pulled from the myth what related to our present-
day lives, and from this created the modern-day
scenes.
We feel this is a transitional myth dealing with
the eventual downfall of a matriarchy and the establishment of the patriarchy. (p. 1)

The play is logically structured on the basis of the
example drawn from mythology. Aristotle explains that an
example functions through induction and concerns "part to
part, like to like."[17] The passage above indicates that the
example used in the play is the myth and that the modern-
day scenes are "the thing exemplified." The audience is
shown the parallel consequences of male domination as those
consequences occur in both types of scenes.

As the play opens, a ritual dance that celebrates
Demeter, the Mother Goddess, is in progress. Meanwhile,
the abduction of Persephone, Demeter's daughter, is planned
by Zeus and Hades. Hades wants Persephone to be his companion in the lonely underworld, and Zeus agrees to help lure
her because he knows Persephone will eventually reveal "the
mystery of the womb." If Zeus can find out the secrets of
the Mother Goddess he will "increase [his] power over life"
(p. 10). As predicted, Persephone is abducted to the underworld where she becomes the wife of Hades. In her lone-
liness she reveals the secrets of birth, and with this information Zeus is able to take control of the earth. The patriarchy comes into existence and as Demeter prophesized
earlier, "...He [man] will sow seed without consent and
separate women from one another to reserve our power for
his own" (p. 9). The abduction and subsequent rape of
Persephone by Hades is a demonstration of the sexual domination that has become one of the characteristics of patriarchy.

The modern scenes exemplify the use of rape as a
method of patriarchal control. The audience is shown four
instances in which men are forcefully seducing women. In
the first scene, a young man is making obscene advances
toward his date. In the next scene, an old man is moles-
ting an innocent schoolgirl. The third scene shows a rapist
approaching and attacking his victim. Finally, we see a
husband insist that his wife have sexual intercourse with him
even though she doesn't want to. In all of the instances,

the female tries to reject the advances of the men, but the
men have control of the relationship.

Toward the end of the play, RIFT presents the possible alternatives to patriarchal dominance. In one short
scene, an abstract character named RHETORIC offers the
sexual possibilities that a woman can opt for:

> I don't know whether I should be a woman identi-
> fied woman and put all my love and energy into
> just women, or if I should deal with men, because
> they do exist....
> Or maybe I should be bi. Maybe I should
> be bisexual, that would be liberated! (p. 20)

At the very end of the play, there is a scene in which two
women build a fire at a campsite that the script notes explain as "symbolic of burning the past and building a fire of
new power" (p. 28). This is followed by all the actors performing a "future dance" which is supposed to portray a new
and androgynous society. RIFT notes that "the pairing in
the 'future dance' is alternately homosexual, heterosexual,
and bisexual. Both men and women give birth and are born
of each other" as part of the dance movement (p. 28). It
appears that RIFT is calling for a more androgynous society
even though the script notes explain that "Persephones Return
may be an exorcism of the patriarchy," but not necessarily
"an answer to what the future will be" (p. 3). The audience
is left to decide for themselves which course of action they
will follow.

The demonstration of male control through rape is a
violent depiction of power which female audience members
should immediately find repulsive. To aid further in the
arousing of the appropriate emotions, the playwrights de-
liberately portray the characters as opposites. The men
exhibit negative traits which arouse the animosity of the
audience toward those characters. On the other hand, the
women in the play are seen as victims of the enemy. The
audience is apt to take pity on the female characters, and
to see their victimization as evidence of an unjust situation.

The use of characters in this way is similar to the
way in which characters are portrayed in melodrama. The
playwright reduces morality to black and white, and there
is no doubt about which characters stand for a particular
mode of conduct. Robert Heilman says in his book Tragedy
and Melodrama, "...In this structure [melodrama], man is
pitted against a force outside of himself--a specific enemy,
a hostile group, a social force, a natural event, an accident

or coincidence."[18] If we change the words "man" and "himself" to "woman" and "herself," we have an accurate description of Persephones Return, The Johnnie Show, and But What
Have You Done For Me Lately? In each play, a woman is
pitted against a man. This represents women and men as
two opposing groups in real life. By making the characters
into positive and negative types, the authors are able to use
those characters for rhetorical ends.

Karen Malpede's The End of War, first performed in
1977 by Malpede's New Cycle Theater, is very similar to
Persephones Return in construction and theme.[19] Malpede
has selected a historical example rather than a mythological
one, but she conveys the message that war and its consequences (notably rape and plunder) are patriarchal actions
that must be rejected in favor of a society based on a code
of nonviolence.

On a general level, the play may be viewed as an
argument between men and women over the efficacy of war.
The play represents deliberative discourse in which the women
attempt to dissuade the men--the makers of war--from engaging in destruction. Through this opposition in male/female
philosophy, the playwright demonstrates a "pacifist-feminist"
perspective to the audience.[20]

The story concerns Nestor Makhno, the leader of the
anarchist movement in the Ukraine at the time of the Russian
Revolution. Makhno leads the peasants to free the town of
Bol'Shaya from the Whites. Bol'Shaya falls a second time,
but Makhno and his men manage to liberate the Ukraine. A
commune is established, but the hope for peace is short-
lived. Both the Bolsheviks and the Whites assault Makhno and his
people. Makhno is wounded during a battle, but the peasants smug-
gle him out of the Ukraine. Makhno's ex-lover conceals the escape from Trotsky, but his wife refuses to go with him. The wife,
Galina, gives birth in the final scene. The birth, viewed
from the events that preceded it, is a demonstration of the
playwright's feminist philosophy:

> Feminist theater as I practice it is concerned with
> women surviving and creating new and human com-
> munities out of the wreckage of the past.[21]

The first argument over war comes in scene four.
Galina, Voline (a poet and friend of Makhno), and Elena
(Makhno's ex-lover) are waiting together at a campsite.
Galina and Elena engage Voline in a forensic argument in
which the women accuse the poet of glorifying war. Galina
says it is the women who suffer losses in battle but do not

complain in their grief. Elena accuses all poets of using
their art falsely to glorify war.   She uses the example of
the Trojan War, asking, "What if Helen had refused to go
to Troy?" She says, "Homer's epic would have been re-
shaped and all the men who choose to follow violent ways
would have to do so without the poet's praise" (p. 17). Then
she accuses Voline of doing the same thing with this war:

> You've made pain wonderful. You've turned murder
> into fate. You've given permanence to hate. (p. 17)

Voline counters by saying, "What's done becomes the only
pattern that we know; the evil done is all that is passed on"
(p. 18). Elena responds by saying it is their responsibility
to see that the next generation suffers less than they have.
The argument ends with Elena advising, "The equality of
pain should be the sole inequality we know once we trust
that the end of war is worth giving lasting shape to" (p. 18).
     The primary strategy used by the women in this
argument is emotion.   They evoke the negative responses
that coincide with war: hate, fear, grief, despair, and anger.
They accuse men of perpetuating war and make the point
that it is unjust to humanity.   Elena's argument by example
(Homer and the telling of the Trojan War) employs inductive
reasoning.   Homer glorified war; Voline is recording the
events of the Russian Revolution; Voline glorifies war too.
She tries to show Voline that his obligation is to record the
horrors of war so that future generations will make choices
less violent than those who lived before.
     In scenes five and six, the audience is witness to
the rape of women as an ugly consequence of war. The rape
theme runs throughout the play and serves as a metaphor for
the direct oppression of women by men.   The theme arouses
the emotions of the audience; especially the women, who fear
that rape is a possibility for all women. We take pity on the
characters in the play who are victims, and our anger is
aroused at the injustice of the act.
     In scene five, Nestor Makhno goes off with Elena,
his ex-lover, while his wife Galina watches in anger.   She
realizes that her husband, who is also the hero of the peasants, has the power to do whatever he wishes and to be
with whomever he wishes.   Galina is pregnant at this time,
and she feels betrayed and humiliated by Makhno's actions.
The old Mother sings her a song about all men that ends
with "there's no escape from rape, young girl.   There's no
escape from rape" (p. 27).

In the next scene, The Raped Woman relates her
horrible experience during the invasion of Gulai-Polye. The
woman speaks to a man dressed in a priest's robe, as if
she is confessing (perhaps symbolic of the guilt that is always
placed on the woman?). First she testifies that she saw
soldiers repeatedly rape an old woman who died from their
brutality. Next her own child was raped before her eyes:

> She was too small to receive them. One took a
> dagger from under his belt. He sliced open the
> sweet pink flesh between her legs. "Baby, baby,"
> he cried. But she, terrified, could not cry, neither
> could she run. Her strong, young legs lay useless
> under her, split apart by a knife and something
> worse than a knife. (p. 29)

Then the woman gives testimony of her own rape by the same
man who raped her daughter. As she finishes her pitiful con-
fession, the priest himself (who is really a demented man
dressed in holy robes) falls lecherously upon her. Nestor
Makhno pulls the demented man away, and Galina tries to
comfort the victims of battle. Makhno motions Galina away,
and she ironically asks, "Am I any less unclean than the
women who follow behind us [?] Because I went to your bed
willingly did you use me any more lovingly than your enemies
used them [?]" (p. 30).
      In scenes eight and ten, the audience is advised to
reject war and to replace it with a nonviolent society based
on bonding and nurturing. In scene eight, the old Mother,
Galina, and Elena are waiting by a lake while the men are
fighting a battle. The two young women confess their jealousy
of each other as lovers of the same man. The women realize that because of men and their war, women have given up
a life of peace and harmony. The old Mother sings a song
that invites Galina and Elena to transcend the evil and suffering they have experienced as a result of the patriarchy:

> ...this is a night to heal wounds.
> For one moment all is different
> all is changed
> all is as it could have been
> had women not suffered other's pain.
> (p. 38)

A transformation takes place. Now, rather than competing
against each other, Galina and Elena have the strength to
support each other through the ordeal of war.

At the end of the play, it is the women who survive.
Elena has gone to Trotsky to bargain for peace while Nestor
Makhno is smuggled out of the Ukraine. Galina, who is about
to give birth, abandons Nestor to stay behind. She has seen
the reality of the ways of heroes and the consequences they
bring to the lives of their followers. She says, "If everything
that every peasant fought for depends upon the single life of
a single man, it doesn't matter if it's Nestor, Trotsky or
some other crueler than either of them" (pp. 42-43). Galina
decides her only chance for happiness is with her child.

In the last scene, Elena is brought back by the poet
Voline. She has been brutally tortured, but through some
powerful inner will she has survived the injury inflicted upon
her by Trotsky. Through Elena, the playwright expresses
her advice for the future:

> The world will perish in such hands as their's
> [sic].... Man makes his own destiny but he makes
> it only once unless the whole pattern is reversed
> and in each head a wakening occur and in each
> heart a way to love what we most fear is found.
> (p. 47)

And then Galina gives birth. The two women, the poet, and
child are all embraced as the lights dim.

In The End of War, Malpede has relied upon the
example of the Russian Anarchists to dissuade the audience
from accepting the patriarchal institution of war. Within
the example, she has used emotional proof and testimony as
the primary means of demonstrating how women are the
victims of men's actions. The theme that women are op-
pressed through rape is a further demonstration of the way
in which men control the lives of women. As in the three
previous plays, the male and female characters are pitted
philosophically against each other, and the audience is shown
that it is the women who are offering a better, nonviolent
society.

In Chapter One, feminist theatre was defined by
Anselma Dell'Olio as "the study of woman and her sub-human
status in our society." Feminists view the dehumanization of
women as a direct result of the patriarchal system, and this
dehumanization has been used successfully as a theme to
demonstrate the injustice of sexual politics in the plays of
feminist theatre groups. The next two plays, Taking It Off
and Babes in the Bighouse, are representative of this theme.

Taking It Off, by the Rhode Island Feminist Theatre
(RIFT), was first performed in 1973. [22] The action in the
play takes place in the Pleasant Valley Beauty Camp, where
four women have paid a large sum of money to come and
attain their "beauty potential." The staff at Pleasant Valley
is all male and includes the camp director, a psychiatrist,
the recreational director (an ex-Marine), and the chef. As
the story unfolds, it becomes increasingly clear that the staff
and the guests represent opposite ends of a power spectrum.
Not only do the men control the daily lives of the women in
the camp, but they also represent American society in which
men dominate women's personal lives. This is also a play
about sex-role stereotyping in which men and women behave,
look, and think according to social convention.

The power struggle is set up in the first scene when
the camp director (ironically) says, "The more you find out
about Pleasant Valley, the more I'm sure you'll realize that
we hold the key to that secret problem of yours, that secret
something that lies between you and total joy" (p. 1). The
staff then proceeds to humiliate and coerce the guests into
realizing their beauty potential based on "professional opinion."

At the weighing-in, the women strip to their under-
garments while the men become a computer spitting out their
heights, weights, and measurements. When Mrs. Mary
Bartholomew turns out to weigh decidedly more than she
recorded on her application form, the staff begins to force
her into a program that is more than she wants to undertake.
The fact comes out that her husband does not know she is
at the camp, nor does she want to tell him. The psychiatrist,
Mark, starts diagnosing her "situation" and rudely tells her
that deception suggests "some sort of psychological problem"
between husband and wife. Suddenly the staff wants to give
her treatments for body hair, perspiration control, scalp
hygiene, and stamina. Mark deals a final humiliating blow
to Mary (she is still in her underwear) by asking, "Are you
concerned about the difference in the sizes of your breasts?"
(p. 6).

Further dehumanization occurs during the exercise
scene. Dennis, the recreational director, is authoritarian
and still acts like the tough Marine he used to be. He tells
the women to push themselves, but adds, "If you really think
you're not gonna make it then you can stop, but don't be
cheating yourself with a weakling attitude, because hard work
is the only way you're gonna get the body you want" (p. 11).
After a series of calisthenics and races, Dennis has managed
to cause bickering and cheating among the women.

The stereotype of perfect beauty is portrayed in a humorous scene wherein Bill, the chef, is fixing soup. From offstage the women's voices can be heard calling out the ingredients--" long slender thighs, small, even breasts, striking features, small waist, etc." (pp. 15-16). As the women call out the characteristics, Bill pantomines each one and then adds it to the soup. The other male actors add bubbling, gurgling noises until the soup begins to boil. The voices become faster and more intense, then fade out.

The difference in status between staff and guests is obvious at mealtime. The staff eat at a separate table, often after the ladies have finished. Bill fixes the men gourmet meals while the ladies receive "quality" meals without the "quantity" they are used to.

Throughout the play, the psychiatrist, Mark, has a way of starting arguments with the guests and through manipulation, working each one into a state of hysteria. At that point he accuses them of having a serious problem. In one scene, Lucy asks Mark what he thought of a magazine article on vitamins. He dismisses her questions, but she persists. As their argument becomes more heated, two actors wearing overalls come over to Lucy. They proceed to tie her up with a long rope and force her into a very uncomfortable sitting position. Throughout this nonverbal humiliation, Lucy and Mark continue speaking. When Mark accuses her of being distraught, Lucy blurts out:

> Lucy: I'm not distraught. I was only trying to
> have a simple conversation on an equal level
> with you. But you don't seem to...
>
> Mark: Why do you think you're inferior, Mrs. Corel?
> I mean, isn't that what you're really trying
> to tell me--that you can't feel on an equal
> level?
>
> Lucy: No! I'm only--
>
> Mark: I would advise a consultation with me, Mrs.
> Corel. For some reason your weight, your
> marriage--I really don't know yet--but for
> some reason...

Lucy gets the last word in by telling Mark just to forget the whole discussion.

The ultimate humiliation occurs when Mary's husband, Bob, calls her from overseas. In spite of the fact that Mary

paid her own camp fees and did not want her husband to
know where she was, the camp director called him anyway.
It is "standard camp procedure to check with the husband"
about all bills (p. 37). Mary is furious. She also misses
her husband, but suspects that he has taken his secretary
with him to Europe. Mary's frustration over the camp experience explodes into rage when Bob calls to say he is
staying over three more weeks and admits he is with his
secretary. He lashes out at Mary telling her that she is
"irrational" and out of control. Mary tells him that he
"makes her sick." Bob counters with:

> It's sick to take three thousand dollars and spend
> it at a fat farm just because your self-respect
> depends on losing two inches at the waist. If you
> can't be happy without looking like Miss America,
> and chaining me to you like a pet puppy, then I
> feel sorry for you. (pp. 39-40)

Mary squares off with the camp staff and tells them
all what she thinks of them and their camp. She demands a
tuition refund and threatens to leave the following morning.
The men tell her she is rude, hysterical, and throwing a
temper tantrum. After she leaves, the men all agree that
she's "a real bitch."
Still feeling like she has regained some of her "free
spirit," Mary returns to the dorm and incites the other
women to raid the kitchen. The women sarcastically offer
a toast to Mark--"Up yours, Harrington!"--and mimic all
the other members of the staff (p. 49). The play ends with
the women realizing that they are locked into their roles and
that achieving their beauty potential is a necessary part of
their social function. Lucy hits the point with the closing
lines: "Well, I happen to be married to a rather important
doctor, and I....I just have certain reasons to look my best
....I have to be on constant call--for my husband" (p. 53).
RIFT has used ethos, the credibility of characters,
to demonstrate the humiliation and dehumanization of women
as a result of the patriarchy. The men are authoritarian,
rude, manipulative, and ill-willed. The women are shown,
once again, as the victims of an unjust system. The audience
is persuaded to take pity on the women and their plight, while
feeling angry toward the agents of injustice.
Taking It Off functions as deliberative discourse as
far as its message to reject male control is demonstrated,
but as in But What Have You Done For Me Lately?, the
audience is not offered an alternative. The characters in

the play realize that trying to achieve the beauty potential
brings unhappiness and frustration, but they remain locked
into this male-defined goal at the end of the play. The wom-
en are still part of conventional society and fall into the
trappings of the sexual roles, even though it appears that
RIFT is urging the female audience members to take more
control over their own lives. Mary is the only character in
the play who does reject the status quo, but the audience is
not shown any of her decisions after she leaves the camp.
RIFT leaves it up to each person in the audience to make
a decision about who will ultimately control their personal
lives.

Like Taking It Off, Megan Terry's Babes in the Bighouse depicts the dehumanization of women as a result of
social convention.[23] The women in Babes are not in a weight-
loss camp, but in a prison. While the action of both plays
takes place in a controlled environment, only the women in
Taking It Off seem to have a way out.

Babes in the Bighouse depicts existing conditions in a
women's prison and is called a "documentary" by the playwright. Since no real solution or advice is offered, the
message is more like an epideictic speech in which the (patriarchal) system is blamed for the dehumanization of the
women prisoners.[24] The negative aspects of prison life are
magnified to such a point that the audience members are
induced to agree with the playwright's point of view.

The prisoners and the prison staff represent opposite
levels of the social structure. The prisoners are considered
social deviants and are subordinate to the prison staff. The
staff represents acceptable social norms and have, as their
primary concern, the transformation of the prisoners into
proper ladies so that they can "be useful members of society"
upon release from prison. Such rehabilitation, however,
hardly seems likely in view of the dehumanizing procedures
that are shown throughout the play.

Prison life is dominated by rules, and daily life in
the prison is punctuated by bells. Prisoners are counted
several times a day. The scenes that show new prisoners
being processed on arrival reveal the control which the state
exerts over everything--dress, activities, mealtimes, job
assignments, showers, even talking. If the rules are broken,
the prisoners are thrown into solitary confinement or forced
to do hard labor.

The prisoners react with violence, vulgar language,
and lesbian behavior. The lesbian theme runs throughout
the play in direct contrast to the behavior advocated by the
prison staff. Lesbian acts are used by the prisoners as a

means to build some kind of human relationship in an environment that denies a woman the right to become intimate with
others on any level. Those who engage in lesbianism run the
risk of severe punishment if caught. This is demonstrated
in a scene in which a character named Teresa is caught
making advances to another woman in the shower. She is
punished by a doctor who injects her with a serum that causes
severe convulsions and violent pain. The doctor tells her to
learn to control herself so that when she gets out of prison
she "can get herself a husband and settle down and live like
a normal human being" (act II, p. 26). When Teresa rejects
the doctor's advice, he threatens her with more injections
and asks:

> Do you promise you will become a feminine person,
> demure and self-controlled? To smile whenever
> you see me walk by? To control your temper and
> learn to walk like a sexy woman? (act II, p. 27)

Teresa does promise to "become a feminine person," but the
very next scene in the play shows that the lesbian behavior
of the prisoners is a conscious choice to defy the code of
sexual politics. A prisoner named Ronnie proclaims:

> I chose to be gay. I chose a woman to defy the
> man. It was a political act and it was a sex act.
> (act II, p. 28)

One interpretation of the lesbian theme might be that the
playwright is calling for lesbianism in real life as an alternative to the heterosexual relationships of the patriarchy.
This would certainly be one way in which women could break
away from sexual control by men.
        At the end of the play, the prisoners are all singing
a song called "Pardon Me." The ending seems somewhat
dated (even inappropriate) because the song refers to Gerald
Ford's pardon of Richard Nixon and the light sentences received by other Watergate criminals. The characters simply
sing, "You'll feel glad. If you'll pardon me. Pardon me.
Pardon me" (act II, p. 35).
        Megan Terry has written a play that persuades by
emphasizing the negative conditions of life in a women's
prison. She has shown the audience the violence and base-
ness of the life-style and the unjust behavior of those who
run the prison. The women recieve ill treatment rather than
attempts at rehabilitation because society is based on the
patriarchal notion of sexual politics.

Babes in the Bighouse invites comparison with Terry's
Keep Tightly Closed in a Cool Dry Place.[25] Keep Tightly
Closed, written in 1965, concerns three men who are serving
life sentences for the murder of one of the men's wives.
The action takes place in a jail cell. The setting has been
described by Sidney Walter as "a metaphor for the prisons
in which we are all confined."[26] It seems that Babes in the
Bighouse is really not much more than the female version of
Keep Tightly Closed. The agent of oppression differs slightly;
in Keep Tightly Closed, society imposes the confinement of
the prisoners, but in Babes it appears that men (the patriarchy)
are responsible for the restrictions placed on women's lives.

The last two plays in this chapter are of the deliberative type of rhetoric and offer the audience a solution to the
problem of patriarchy. Although both solutions are weak, the
audience is at least offered an alternative to a corrupt system.

How to Make a Woman by Bobbi Ausubel (with Stan
Edelson) was first performed by Caravan Theatre in 1967,
and is considered one of the first plays of women's liberation.[27]
The play concerns two women shopping for a new dress. During the course of the play, the different "dresses" that each
try on represent the different roles a female plays during
her lifetime. The dress shop is run by two archetypal men,
the Hunter and the Wolf, and they are assisted by a mannequin
who represents society's "mechanized women."

The play is almost entirely fantasy and abstraction,
but the roles the women are asked to play cannot be mistaken.
Aili and Mary are shown in such roles as a demure child,
a submissive wife, an adultress, a mother, and a tyrant
wife. In the end, Mary becomes another mannequin, but
Aili refuses to be what society asks of her. When she is
pressured to choose, Aili firmly says, "No. I want a different dress. These designs are all yours and not mine"
(pp. 56-57). To this the Hunter replies:

> All right you don't want our dresses. (to audience)
> There are plenty of women out there who do. I
> am a man. A bastion. The prime mover. The
> engineer of humanity. (p. 57)

Aili screams and runs out of the shop, asking the women in
the audience to break out of the shop with her.

When How to Make a Woman first went into production,
none of the members of Caravan (male or female) had heard
of "Women's Liberation," so the play was not originally
written as a feminist drama. However some people in the
women's movement heard about (or possibly saw) the play,

and it was booked by Mary Daly in conjunction with a women's
liberation group. At that performance, a discussion was
started after the show, and discussions became an integral
part of performance after that time.[28] In the 1970 edition
of the play, which has been used here, Bobbi Ausubel described the discussion format:

> Following performances the cast and crew joined
> the audience to discuss the play and the issues it
> presents. We found the discussion most fruitful
> when we separated into smaller groups of all men
> and all women and ended by bringing these groups
> together, sometimes as a whole, sometimes divid-
> ing into mixed groups of about ten people, to talk
> about what they had discussed separately. The
> subject of Women's Liberation was introduced, very
> often as a reply to the often-raised point made by
> the audience that the play offers no "solutions."
> (p. i) [29]

The fact that Aili rejects society's stereotype of a
woman is in itself a partial solution. The audience is not
shown what happens after she leaves the dress shop, but
they do know she has realized she must resist the injustice
of patriarchy if she is to become an autonomous human being.
The discussion offers a rational resolution to the persuasive
process. The suggestion to participate in the women's movement offers a future action by which the audience can undo
the damage of sexual politics. Caravan intended this solution
for both women and men, for the play demonstrates that men
are as locked into sex roles as women are. The ethical
proof demonstrated through the negative traits of the Hunter
and the Wolf is designed as much to show men that they
need to change as it is to show everyone that men are the
oppressors.

The last play in the sexual politics category is different from all the others because it confronts the issue of
male control with an all-female cast. Like the preceding
play, Paper Weight offers a solution to outside domination,
but we never directly see the men who are responsible for
the inequitable working conditions of the women.

Members of the Rhode Island Feminist Theatre (RIFT)
wrote Paper Weight in 1979 to demonstrate the plight of
women office workers. [30] The setting is the records department of a large, metropolitan insurance company. The work
is routine and boring, and slowly we find out the women's
gripes: the annoying requests for coffee by the managers,

stories of sexual harassment, low wages for a heavy work-
load, unfair promotion criteria, a dull working environment,
and no job satisfaction.

When a new manager arrives, the clerks are surprised
to find that it is a woman. Their hopes for change ("maybe
she'll be more sympathetic to our problems") quickly vanish
when the new manager turns out to be more rule-oriented than
the old boss. What becomes clear is that in order to suc-
ceed, the new manager must show the corporation that she
can control her subordinates as effectively as any male manager. Thus, she is really a victim of the patriarchal system.
The clerks are treated unfairly because the corporate rules
are unfair and inflexible.

The test of the new manager comes when Melissa Mae
requests to leave work early to attend her son's speech
therapy sessions. Rather than working through an informal
network in personnel, the manager insists that the issue be
decided by the Policy Committee. The committee turns down
the request, and Melissa Mae is forced to quit. All the
clerks are bitter that the company showed no compassion for
a five-year employee. The manager's only excuse is, "We
have to become a part of the system by cooperating with the
establishment" (p. 53).

At the end of the play, the rest of the clerks have
drawn up a petition to request representation on the Policy
Committee. They realize that it's too late to do anything
for Melissa Mae, but if they want to protect themselves in
the future, the petition may be the key to beating the system.

In Paper Weight, RIFT has demonstrated the unfair-
ness of the patriarchal system in an example drawn from
corporate life. The audience is advised to reject the system
in favor of a process that treats men and women on a more
equal basis. Of all the plays in this chapter, Paper Weight
is probably the least feminist in perspective. It is true that
the clerks in this play are similar to women in real life who
hold the majority of clerk positions. It is also true that the
problems faced by the characters (requests for coffee, sexual
harassment, etc.) are specific to female office workers.
However, the problem of an inflexible company that treats
its employees unfairly seems to be generalizable to almost
any bureaucratic setting. Perhaps RIFT's play is more a
plea for human equality in the work sphere than it is a request for female liberation from the patriarchy.[31]

The plays in this category, "sexual politics," have
sought to persuade audiences that male domination is morally
wrong and unjust to its female victims. The feminist theatre
groups have appealed to the audience's sense of what is right

or wrong at the instinctive level. Aristotle makes a distinction between right and wrong in relation to two levels of law-- man-made and universal. He explains:

> Justice and injustice admit of a twofold distinction
> with reference both to the laws and to the persons
> affected. I mean that law is either particular or
> universal; by 'particular' law I mean that which an
> individual community lays down for itself (a law
> partly unwritten, partly written); and by 'universal'
> law I mean the law of nature. For there is a
> natural and universal notion of right and wrong,
> one that all men instinctively apprehend, even when
> they have no mutual intercourse nor any compact.
>   To be wronged is to suffer injustice at the hands
> of the voluntary agent.... And the person wronged
> must be harmed, and harmed against his will.[32]

The plays in this chapter tell the audience that war, abortion laws, television advertising, women's prisons, rape, control of a woman's personal life and physical appearance, and corporate policy are all male forms of sexual control that are wrong. The women who are the victims of injustice suffer physical, mental, and emotional harm against their will.

Most of the plays in this category function (either implicitly or explicitly) as deliberative discourse. The drama advises the audience to reject the sexual ideology that governs human interaction, and in some instances calls for a matriarchal society as an appropriate replacement for the patriarchy. Most future action, however, is left up to individual members of the audience.

The theatre groups that produced these plays have relied heavily on credibility and emotion as proof for the cases they present. The characters are reduced to types and are morally pitted against each other. It is clear that men are the enemies and the voluntary agents of female oppression. The women are usually shown as victims who suffer from constant dehumanization at the hands of patriarchy. The emotional proof is centered around the negative consequences suffered by the characters in the plays that produce the appropriate feelings of pity and indignation in the audience. The characters suffer shame, fear, anger, and enmity as a result of patriarchal actions such as a rape and abortion laws that deny a woman control over her body.

Logical proof is secondary to emotional proof and the use of credibility in these plays. Several of the dramas

(The End of War, Paper Weight, Persephones Return) are
based on an example from which the audience draws conclusions about the general state of society. Two plays (But
What Have You Done For Me Lately?, The Johnnie Show)
employ role reversal as a rhetorical strategy wherein the
men suddenly have typical patriarchal words and actions
turned against them. The strategy works to help male audience members empathize with the female position, and works
effectively as a jolting, dramatic technique to make a point.
      Not all of the plays are persuasive in an obvious way.
Babes in the Bighouse serves as a metaphor for the "prisons"
in which women are confined as a result of male domination.
The play is a depiction of existing conditions, and offers no
advice to the audience. Likewise, Paper Weight functions
more as a story about victims of corporate bureaucracy
rather than a persuasive argument against sexual politics in
the office.
      The plays in this chapter are aimed at a mixed au-
dience and serve to describe the problem (including "naming
the enemy"), ask the men to make changes in themselves
and their treatment of women, and call for women to reject
an oppressive system. Many of the early plays (How to
Make a Woman, But What Have You Done For Me Lately?)
have an angry and accusatory tone, while others (Taking It
Off, The Johnnie Show) use humor as a way of adding comic
relief to a problem situation. In the next chapter a very
different group of plays will be examined. We will be turning toward messages designed for women only, and will address the way in which women define themselves as human
beings.

NOTES

1. S.H. Butcher, trans., Aristotle's Poetics (New York:
   Hill and Wang, 1961), p. 62. By extension, the
   six parts of tragedy have been applied by theatre
   scholars to all types of drama.

2. Ibid., p. 93.

3. Sam Smiley, The Drama of Attack (Columbia: University of Missouri Press, 1972), pp. 6, 18.

4. Ibid., "Rhetorical Principles in Didactic Drama,"
    The Quarterly Journal of Speech, 57 (1971), pp.
    147-52.

5. Smiley, op.cit., p. 15.

6. This author is distinguishing a belief from a con-
    viction by defining a belief as a predisposition to
    action which is subject to change, and a conviction
    as a strongly held or fixed belief which is more
    difficult to change. For an interesting discussion
    of the organization and function of belief systems,
    see Milton Rokeach, Beliefs, Attitudes, and Values
    (San Francisco: Jossey-Bass, 1975).

7. Lane Cooper, trans., The Rhetoric of Aristotle
    (Englewood Cliffs, N.J.: Prentice-Hall, 1932), pp.
    17ff. All further references to the Rhetoric are
    from the Cooper edition.

8. Ibid., pp. 8-9.

9. Kate Millett, Sexual Politics (New York: Ballantine
    Books, 1969), p. 31.

10. Ibid., p. 33.

11. Myrna Lamb, But What Have You Done For Me
    Lately?, in The Mod Donna and Scyklon Z (New
    York: Pathfinder Press, 1971), pp. 143-166. All
    further references to this work appear in the text.

12. This line of argument is an effective choice for
    forensic argument, in which it is the speaker's goal
    to completely discredit the accused. See Cooper, p.
    162.

13. Cooper, op.cit., pp. 18, 73-78.

14. See Brenda Hancock, "Affirmation by Negation In
    the Women's Liberation Movement," The Quarterly
    Journal of Speech, 58 (1972), pp. 264-71.

15. Rhode Island Feminist Theatre, The Johnnie Show
    (Providence: n.p., 1974). All further references
    to this work appear in the text.

16. Ibid., Persephones Return (Providence: n.p., 1975).
All further references to this work appear in the
text. ʼ Note: The apostrophe in Persephone's has
been omitted in the copy of the play this author
received from RIFT. Acknowledgement of the
omission here should suffice, so the insertion of "sic"
will not be used hereafter.

17. Cooper, op.cit., pp. 14, 148-49.

18. Robert Heilman, Tragedy and Melodrama (Seattle:
Univ. of Washington Press, 1968), p. 79.

19. Karen Malpede, The End of War, New York, revised edition, 1982. Unpublished manuscript received from Malpede, April 1982. All further
references to this work appear in the text.

20. Malpede's philosophy is described by Patti Gillespie
in Gillespie's article, "A Listing Of Feminist Theaters," Theatre News, 10, No. 2 (Nov. 1977), p. 24.

21. Ibid., p. 24.

22. Rhode Island Feminist Theatre, Taking It Off
(Providence: Hellcoal Press, 1973). All further
references to this work appear in the text.

23. Megan Terry, Babes in the Bighouse (Omaha: Omaha
Magic Theatre Press, 1974). All further references
to this work appear in the text.

24. This author has used the term "epideictic" in a
broad sense, and has applied it primarily to the
structure of the drama. Although Aristotle related
the term to discourse about people, he also said
it "does not always concern a human being or a
god, for often enough it is applied to inanimate
things, or to some insignificant animal" (Cooper,
p. 46). This author uses the word to apply to
plays that either censure or praise institutions.
In Babes, the playwright censures patriarchy as an
evil institution in society. Sam Smiley says, "In
the twentieth century, most epideictic speeches
are written to praise [or blame] a man, an organization, and institution, or a way of life" (Drama
of Attack, p. 70).

25. Megan Terry, Four Plays (New York: Touchstone, 1966).

26. Sidney Walter, "Notes for the Firehouse Theatre Production, " in Four Plays, p. 206.

27. Bobbi Ausubel, How to Make a Woman, Boston, 1970. Unpublished manuscript received from Ausubel, June 1982. All further references to this work appear in the text.

28. The information about the play's evolution into a "feminist" work comes from an interview with the members of Caravan by staff members of the journal Female Liberation. Photocopy of the interview received from Bobbi Ausubel,   March 1982.

29. The importance of the discussion period as part of the rhetorical process is also discussed in Chapters Two and Six.

30. Rhode Island Feminist Theatre, Paper Weight, Providence, 1979. Unpublished manuscript received from RIFT, December 1981. All further references to this work appear in the text.

31. This idea was brought up at a discussion following a performance of Paper Weight. One of the comments about the character of the manager was that, like any new manager climbing the corporate ladder, she "sold out" to the corporation in order to make personal gains. Had the employees under this manager been male, they would have been just as powerless as the female characters in the play. Janet Buchwald, dir., Paper Weight, by the Rhode Island Feminist Theatre, Educational Center for the Arts, New Haven, 21 November 1981.

32. Cooper, op.cit., pp. 73-74.

Chapter Four
THE WOMAN-IDENTIFIED WOMAN

The six plays that are the subject of analysis in this
chapter clearly differ from those in the previous chapter in
both audience orientation and intent. While the plays of sexual
politics speak to both men and women, the plays here speak
primarily to women. The central idea that guides the action of
these plays is that women must redefine themselves in terms
of female attributes rather than through a heretofore accepted
male definition. A corollary idea is that once a woman accepts
the new definition of herself she can function in a positive, autonomous manner.

The problem of female definition is inherently difficult
for women to deal with because historically women have been
defined by men and in relation to men. Our Judeo-Christian
heritage tells us that God took a rib from Adam and made a
woman in order to provide a helpmate for Adam. The Bible
establishes a definition of woman as one who is a helper or
helpful companion to man. A woman thus identifies her role
in relation to the one she serves. When God discovered that
Eve had eaten the forbidden fruit of Eden, he punished her with
the promise that "I will greatly multiply thy sorrow and thy con-
ception; in sorrow thou shalt bring forth children; and thy desire shall be to thy husband, and he shall rule over thee"
(Genesis 3:16). Woman has been condemned from the beginning to a subservient role that has led to countless unfulfilled
lives and the status of subhumanity.

Simone de Beauvoir's perceptive study, The Second Sex,
establishes the concept of the Self and the Other.[1] The Self is
man and the Other is woman. The Self is the locus of definition
of the human being, and "thus humanity is male and man defines
woman not in herself but as relative to him; she is not regarded
as an autonomous being."[2] This dichotomy between man (the
Self) and woman (the Other) implies a complex set of negative
characteristics that are attributed to the woman. A woman is
subordinate, dependent, and herself a negative entity, while
man is dominant, autonomous, and exists as a positive force
in the universe.

The feminists involved in the most recent surge of
the women's movement have taken a step beyond de Beauvoir's
careful analysis of the problem. Not content with a description of the negative lot cast to women, modern feminists have
urged women to look upon themselves from a new point of
view. This new perspective involves seeing woman as a positive force, transcending the Other and taking the Self as the
central position from which to identify the female human being. Thus, woman is relative to herself and not dependent
upon an identification related in any way to man. This concept of relating the female existence to other females is
known as the woman-identified woman. Feminists advocating
this point of view call upon women, and women alone, to
establish what is a very basic answer to a largely metaphys-
ical question:

> Only women can give each other a new sense of
> self. That identity we have to develop with refer-
> ence to ourselves, and not in relation to men.
>   Together we must find, reinforce and validate
> our authentic selves. As we do this, we confirm
> in each other that struggling incipient sense of
> pride and strength, the divisive barriers begin to
> melt, we feel this growing solidarity with our sis-
> ters. 3

The new identification also implies, at least according to
this quoted passage, that the transformation from the negative to the positive will be accompanied by the establishment
of sisterhood among women. The resulting power obtained
from sisterhood is viewed as an essential tool for both individual and social change.
    The new sense of self that women are looking for is
not something to be gained necessarily by engaging in group
consciousness-raising, nor by establishing a matriarchal society, nor by throwing out the men altogether! The process
of establishing the new identity begins with introspection on
the part of every woman. All women must engage in self-
discovery, "a process that is at once painful and at the same
time liberating."4 As each individual woman is freed from
the identity of the past, she contributes to the liberation of
all women.
    Feminist theatre groups have taken on part of the
responsibility of advocating a redefinition of woman and pro-
moting sisterhood. Many of the plays depict the "tortuous
journey" of self-discovery, but all of them convey the message that a woman-identified woman is a catalyst for positive
change.

The plays that belong to this category are structurally different from the plays in the preceding chapter. The authors deal with the female psyche, and very often use nonlinear or experimental techniques to convey the emotional and psychological development of the characters. Action does not necessarily have a logical, cause-to-effect sequence of incidents. The plays tend to be episodic. The characters often reveal their inner state through monologues that are spoken directly to the audience. In many instances, the characters that appear in one part of a drama may not appear again, and so that character does not have an ongoing relationship with other characters in the play. For all of these reasons, the reader is advised to try to get a feel for the emotional quality of the play rather than to try to follow a story line.

Calliope Feminist Theatre in Hartford, Connecticut, has consistently produced drama that emphasizes "powerful, positive images of women."[5] One recent play, Make Up by Mother Nature, performed in February 1982, carries the audience along on one of the journeys of self-discovery that lead to a new identity for the characters in the drama.

The play is divided into three sections. Part I is a satirical depiction of female characteristics that most people react to negatively. The scene is structured like a game show in which female contestants are to "name their shame." Most of the shame is centered around the female body, which is ugly, overweight, or exhibits some other defect that (male) society identifies as unsightly, and which provides the basis for the rejection of the woman. Calliope relies on emotional argument to make the point. While the satirical style allows the audience to laugh, the underlying emotions that are aroused include shame, indignation, and pity. The audience should be asking themselves why they must be ashamed of their bodies, or why they must judge themselves according to criteria that men have set up to judge the worth of others.

In part II, the audience is aroused to a state of anger. A scene dramatizes the powerlessness of women by using the portrayal of an ill-willed gynecologist and his helpless patient. At this point, Calliope relies on the use of character portrayal as a rhetorical strategy. The gynecologist, Dr. Ben Dover, is depicted as a self-centered man who acts maliciously toward his patient, a woman lying prone on an examining table. The doctor is disgusted by the woman's physical ailments and does not act interested in helping her. When she questions his prescriptions, he silences her. The humiliation of the patient by the malevolent doctor is designed to arouse the audience's anger toward Dr. Dover and its pity

for the woman. The audience is undoubtedly outraged that
the male doctor has complete control over his patient's internal condition, and that ailments related to the female re-
productive organs are considered repulsive.

Both parts I and II of the play depict the negative aspects of being female if one defines femaleness by male standards. But in part III, a transformation in the message and
tone of the play takes place. A second scene at the gynecologist's office shows a woman who is knowledgeable about
her body and determined to put Dr. Dover in his place. The
scene is constructed as a forensic argument in which the
woman accuses the doctor of a false diagnosis and has tape-
recorded evidence of his ill treatment of other patients. She
informs him of her intent to report him to Women Against
Medical Abuse, the AMA, and the County Medical Board.
The doctor's guilt is proven by the witnesses' taped testimony,
and the audience is induced to agree based on the doctor's
treatment of the patient seen in part II of the play.

At the end of the play, the cast and audience join
together to recite a poem called "We the Woman of the Earth."
The lines in the poem affirm Calliope's intent to promote
"the empowerment of body, mind, and soul through sisterhood, music, spirituality, and self-love."6 The sisterhood
among women is depicted through a sense of togetherness
that is described in the poem--"We are the power, we are
the connection." As the audience recites with the members
of Calliope, they are brought together and made to feel confident that women can, indeed, see themselves as substantive
human beings who need not be ashamed of their inherent
makeup.

The journey of self-discovery on which Calliope has
led its audience is largely emotional. The appeals to the
audience members' sense of self-esteem and worth are apparent in the transformation process. The women in the
play experience powerful emotions of shame, fear, and indignation. These are ultimately transformed into a positive
identity which the audience is invited to share.

Martha Boesing's Love Song for an Amazon, first
performed by At the Foot of the Mountain in 1976, is described by Boesing as "a celebration and ritual enactment
of [women's] friendship--the multiple masks and the deep
bonding."7 The play is nonlinear and has a ceremonial
quality to it. Rhetorically, this one-act play is akin to an
epideictic speech in which the many characteristics of a
woman are identified for the audience. The composite identity of a woman is portrayed by two characters, Rose and

Aisha, who interact with each other as they play many roles:
childhood playmates, lovers, mother and daughter, Amazons,
and prophetesses. The character transformations are sometimes difficult to follow, so the audience must carefully follow the change in vocabulary and language choices. In performance, the vocal tones of the actors would probably also
serve as clues to character changes. The rhetorical response
that the play arouses in the audience is the acceptance of the
woman-identified woman concept and the resulting sisterhood
that is possible through a committed friendship between women.

As the two characters transform themselves into the
roles just described, the audience is exposed to a number
of traits that characterize the female personality. As children, women are taught to share, to be nice, to be ashamed
of wrongdoing, to accept limitations imposed by others, to
be afraid of war and violence, to tend their dolls. As youth,
women are subject to secrets, competition with other women,
dreams, and passion, but are also capable of stealing and
enjoying the advances of other females.

When the characters transform into Amazons at the
end of the play, they use a pile of rocks to build a structure.
This represents both a temple to honor women and a new
structuring of society Rose and Aisha envision a community of women in which there is no fighting or competition.
When they realize that their matriarchal society will be subject to invasion by men, they decide they will have to take
their message of a female-defined future to both men and
women before it can be accepted. Both sing, "It won't be
long now, sister, won't be long," as the curtain falls. The
vision of a future society that is characterized by female
attributes (passivity, nonviolence, etc.) is offered to the
audience as an outcome for those women (and men) who
choose to bond together.

The rhetorical strategy that Boesing uses in this play
is a depiction of the female character (ethos) in a sensitive,
positive manner. The audience is persuaded to accept their
own femaleness (in all its aspects) as a result of the be-
lievability of the characteristics portrayed by Rose and Aisha.
Note that the use of ethos is not through Rose and Aisha
themselves, but through the composite set of female traits
that Rose and Aisha demonstrate, for the play is abstract,
without any concrete development of plot or character. It
is simply a portrayal of an idea--female identity in the context of women's friendship, rather than female identity through
a male-female relationship.

In the following two full-length plays the idea of an
inward journey toward self-discovery is very pronounced.

The emotional and psychological aspects of the discovery are portrayed through a technique known as personality fragmentation.[8] In both plays, the central character is represented by two actors. One role is the woman as her present self. The other role is the woman as a child. Through the child, the audience sees why the woman is struggling to face a present-- and possibly a future--that she has not been conditioned to deal with. Also common to both plays is the use of a mother character. Her presence provides a further rationale for the woman's difficulty with accepting herself as a female.

Focus on Me!, written by Bobbi Ausubel and first performed by Caravan Theatre in 1974, is the story of a filmmaker named Toni.[9] She wants to make a film about a strong woman ("based on the spirit of the Amazon"), but is unable to "find images for her" (act I, p. 4). As Toni searches for the appropriate images, she undergoes her own search for self-identity as a woman. The playwright's message to the audience is that women must accept all aspects of their femaleness (even those aspects considered weak) in order to function as whole, autonomous people. Rhetorically, the message is conveyed using both emotional and logical proof. The stirring up on the emotions dominates as Toni confronts her own fear and anger throughout the play.

The playing area is divided into three distinct spaces. One space belongs to a fantasy child (Toni's alter ego), another space belongs to Toni's mother, and the third space is Toni's film studio. Action that takes place in the child's area or the mother's space is indicative of action that is going on inside Toni's head. Action that takes place in the film studio is indicative of present reality.

In the scenes with the fantasy child, Toni rejects the suggestions of the child again and again. The child asks to be bathed and to be pushed on a swing. Toni rejects these pleas for a demonstration of her nurturing abilities. The child is shown nursing two dolls and says to Toni, "Film me" (act I, p. 18). Toni rejects the image, turns to the audience, and asks, "Is it too late to make my Amazon woman a mother?" (act I, p. 18). As the fantasy child continues to ask to be mothered, Toni's anger toward her own mother and childhood intensifies.

In the scenes in which the mother character appears and tries to tell Toni what to do, Toni vehemently rejects her. Toni also rejects her own role as a mother. Toni has a daughter named Karrie, who in one scene says to Toni, "You should stay home more like the other mothers do." Toni responds, "I can't. I don't want to be like the other mothers" (act I, p. 13).

In another scene the fantasy child acts out her ambition to be a fireman, an astronaut, and the queen of the jungle. Each time her ambitions are quelled by male voices that tell her she doesn't fit the role. The child insists she can do it, but Toni, like male society, won't accept it. Toni is reduced to a state of complete frustration. She knows she wants to find an image of a strong woman, but nothing seems to fit. Finally Toni confronts herself in a monologue:

> You have to be big and fight back.... Fight back.
> I am crushing me. I am. I am. Focus on me!
> I have burned away all my femaleness...with my
> anger I can destroy everyone! (act II, p. 18)

In the end, Toni comes to the realization that even the Amazon can "stumble," but a woman who can accept all aspects of being female is stronger and leads a more fulfilling life.

While Toni's emotional journey is stirring up the feelings of the audience members, there is a logical argument simultaneously at work in the play. The argument is one of incentive, which Aristotle explains as follows:

> Here you consider the incentives and deterrents
> as the motives people have for doing or avoiding
> acts in question. These are the conditions which,
> according as they are for or against us, make us
> act or refrain from action. [10]

The incentive for Toni (and the audience) to work through the identity crisis is a character in the play named Nina. Nina first appears in Toni's studio asking for a job as a production assistant. She tells Toni that she just left her home, her husband--everything that was part of her life in which she was subordinate to a man. Nina has brought her daughter with her and now plans to support them both with the job she hopes to get at Toni's studio. Toni hires Nina, and not only does Nina help with making the film, but she serves as an incentive for Toni to face her own problems.

Nina's positive attitude toward the complex personality of a female helps Toni to see that if she can accept all these competing characteristics she will be a better person. Some of the competing roles and characteristics that Nina has worked through include: wanting to have a career in a man's world, wanting to be a mother, wanting to be nurtured herself, feeling strong and vulnerable at the same time, enjoying the tenderness of her child, and feeling confused and happy about leaving her husband behind. Nina shows Toni that it is foolish to reject the characteristics of womanhood that society has deemed weak or undesirable, for the gains of being an emotional individual outweigh the losses.

In Focus On Me!, Ausubel has lead the audience through a woman's emotional struggle to accept herself as a woman-identified woman. In the fantasy scenes with the child and mother, the audience is shown, through emotional proofs, the pain and denial of not being able to deal with the expectations of the female role. The character of Nina provides the audience with the incentive to complete the journey. The positive attitudes and apparent well-being of Nina are proof that women need not reject any aspects of their female identity.

Martha Boesing's The Web (1981) focuses on the life of Abigail Sater, a playwright and lecturer on feminist aesthetics.[11] Throughout the play, which uses memory scenes rather than fantasy, Abigail is confronted with the meaning of her life. The scenes shift from past to present to weave a "web" of events that Abigail tries to explain rationally. All of the events have to do with Abigail's relationship with her family. The scenes from the distant past involve her mother, brother, aunt, uncle, and cousin. In these scenes, Abigail is played by another actor representing a character named Abby. In the scenes portraying the present or recent past, Abigail plays herself. Her husband and uncle are in many of these scenes, and she talks frequently on the telephone to a daughter (whom the audience never sees). As the scenes occur, the audience becomes aware that Abigail is obsessed with trying "to make sense out of everything that happens" to her. She tells the audience right away, "I cling to the neurotic belief that if I could understand what events mean, then I could stop obsessing about them" (act I, p. 1). By the end of the play, Abigail has given up her analysis and "moves forward into her life" (act II, p. 29). She comes to the realization that she can accept herself and her family for what they are (and what they are not) without resolving all the uncertainty that exists in life.

Boesing's play emphasizes the psychological over the emotional. Abigail's constant sorting out of events is her way of objectively attacking the problem of self-discovery. This approach contrasts with the emotional trauma that Toni dealt with in Focus On Me!.

What makes this play rhetorical? At first glance there doesn't seem to be a feminist idea central to the plot. Abigail is more a universal than a particular kind (sex) of person. The play seems to be more about a family than an argument for female identity, and in fact, the main idea is presented subtly.[12]

The arguments put forth are in the form of maxims. Aristotle tells us that a maxim is a declarative statement about the general nature of human action or behavior.[13] The maxims in The Web all concern the behavior of females. For example, in one scene Abby tells her Uncle Toby, "I've decided to become a boy." When he asks her why, she responds, "Everybody likes boys better" (act II, p. 25). While some people in the audience may laugh or reject the notion, the general female response will be melancholy agreement. "If only I had been born male" is often the wish of women who find it difficult to be accepted as a female in a man's world. Other maxims that are either declared or implied include: "girls don't know anything" about war and other men's concerns (act I, p. 2); mothers and daughters cannot get along with each other (act I, p. 8); women compete with each other for the attention of others (act I, p. 10); women become "hysterical" and cannot solve problems rationally (act I, p. 10); husbands cannot stand aggressive wives (act I, p. 11); and women have an "abundance of rape fantasies" in their minds (act I, p. 14). Abigail compares these expectations of female behavior with her own feelings about herself and her relationship with other family members.

Six times during the play, Abigail, in her role as a feminist lecturer, walks to a lectern and says, "Tonight's lecture on feminist aesthetics concerns...," and then she delivers a short portion of the lecture. In the first one she compares masculine and feminine aesthetics using the theory of biological determinism:

> The interesting thing about Aristotle's theory of tragedy is its kinship to the male orgasm....Given this classical format of biological determinism, it follows that women's plays could or should be multi-orgasmic in form, small mini-scenes perhaps, coming in waves of emotions, crests and valleys, like the ebb and flow of changing tides, and finally consummating in a sense of nourishment and plentitude, the creation of new life, birth. (Act I, p. 5)

This description of a woman's play fits the structure of The Web, and the playwright's philosophy of feminist (matriarchal) theatre.[14] The Web consists of episodes, similar to those in a Brechtian play, in which the action culminates in Abigail's own "rebirth" as she comes to terms with her identity crisis.

In two other lectures, Abigail speaks metaphorically,
implying a comparison of the human female with a chrysalis
and a spider's web. The chrysalis is the pupa stage of a
moth or butterfly and is symbolic of rebirth. A dictionary
definition says a chrysalis is "anything still in the process
of development."[15] This, of course, is the perfect context
for the play. Abigail is in the process of development throughout the play.

About webs, Abigail says, "Webs are the true maps
of the unconscious. All females spin them. The most notorious
spinner of webs, however, is the female spider." Then she
describes the black widow, who kills and eats her suitors.
At the close of the lecture the audience is left with a maxim:
"there is nothing worse in this universe than a woman without a man" (act II, p. 25). This is ironic, for all three
adult women in the play are either divorced or widowed, and
still manage to survive. Obviously the playwright sets out
to tell the audience that in fact a man is not necessary at
all. Through the use of the maxims the playwright is asking
the audience, "Do you accept the stereotype of the American
woman? What do you want to do about your own identity?"

At the end of the play, Abigail has decided to "shed
her fear as the snake sheds her skin" and move on in her
life (act II, p. 29). The audience is encouraged by Abigail
to explore their own uncertainties, and accept them (or reject them) for what they are, and get on with life. Abigail
seems to exemplify the woman-identified woman because she
acknowledges all of the positive and negative aspects of being
female that she explored in this play. In the end she realizes that the answer to the question she posed earlier, "Who's
in charge anyway?," is "I am!" Every woman is capable
of commanding her life and discovering her own unique identity.

Electra Speaks is the third play in a trilogy called
The Daughters Cycle by Clare Coss, Sondra Segal, and
Roberta Sklar of the Women's Experimental Theatre.[16] The
cycle of plays examines the roles of women in the family.
The first play, Daughters, focuses on the mother-daughter
relationship, while the second play, Sister/Sister, looks at
the development of sister relationships from childhood through
the adult stage. Electra Speaks examines the role of the
daughter and her attempt at self-realization by using the
classic Greek story of Electra of the House of Atreus. The
playwrights explain the purpose of the trilogy:

> Throughout the trilogy we try to develop a fuller
> understanding of the roles and relationships pos-
> sible for women in the family and to reclaim the

women lost within these roles. We attempt to dis-
mantle the past and reconstruct it with our own
women's consciousness, giving a new design to our
present and thereby creating a different future than
the anticipated one. (p. 223)

This commentary gives a clue to the rhetorical structure of Electra Speaks. The play is designed as a deliberative address in which the playwrights use the myths of ancient
Greece to offer advice to a contemporary audience. The
playwrights are exhorting the audience to speak out about
their identity as female beings, to tell how men have violently abused them and ultimately silenced them, and to break
away from the identity that men have given women.

Like Persephones Return, Electra Speaks is a reinterpretation of a myth from a feminist perspective. During
the course of the play, the audience hears the women's side
of the story from Clytemnestra, Iphigenia, Cassandra, Athena,
and Electra. The stories are told in the form of monologues
by each character. The actors assume the role of a Greek
character, and in some instances one actor will transform
into another character or assume more than one role in a
scene. As the women speak, they challenge the portrayal
of themselves by the male storytellers. They argue that
the outward appearance of "the way things happened" is con-
trary to the inward motivation of those who participated in
the events.[17]
When Iphigenia speaks, the audience is told two stories about her sacrifice by Agamemnon. (The story goes
that Agamemnon sent for his daughter so that he could give
her as a bride to a war hero. When Iphigenia arrived, she
was sacrificed in order to insure favorable winds for Agamemnon's
voyage into battle.) The first part of Iphigenia's monologue
tells her own story as history has recorded it. We learn
that the book says Iphigenia somehow accepted her fate to
die, and did so willingly because the act brought great honor
to Greece (pp. 240-41). Then suddenly there is a twist in
the monologue and the audience is told what was left out of
the history books:

They don't say that she tried to fight back.
They don't say what she thought when she
    realized that her father was going to
    murder her.
We don't know anything about her.
Everything is what they say.
We don't know the ways in which she resisted.
(p. 241)

According to a text notation, "they say" represents "the patriarchal voice" (p. 240)   What we see here is a refutation of
the male telling of the myth and a reinterpretation from a
feminist point of view.   The audience is shown that the women's
feelings in this story have been silenced by the storytellers,
and that ultimately the inner thoughts of all women have been
stifled when the man's best interest is in question.
     As the play proceeds, all the women of the House of
Atreus reveal to the audience how the men acted out of their
own self-interest, while the women were abused and used as
objects to help the men reach their own selfish goals.   Under-
neath the outward silence, the women experience violent inward emotions and thoughts, and they wish to tell their side
of the story.
     When Clytemnestra reveals her story, the audience
learns of all her rage and anger built up over the time that
she has been used (and abused) as sustenance for the patriarchy by Agamemnon and Aegisthus:

> Nurtured by woman as food, he creates
> he creates his institutions
> religion family law
> philosophy education
> at night he sucks her titty
> by day he wreaks his vengeance
> this baby man hates his mommy
> what he does in the world
> is the proof
> this baby man hates his mommy
> his need his need his need (p. 234)

This passage serves as a strong argument to accuse men of
objectifying women and sexually abusing them, while at the
same time depending upon them for physical gratification and
for the female's ability to bear their progeny.   The world
revolves around the needs of men, yet it is the women who
provide the means of support for the patriarchy.   The playwrights are urging the audience to reject the patriarchy, to
speak out against the abuse they endure, and to look else-
where for identity.
     It is through the character of Electra that the play-
wrights show what happens when a woman dares to speak, to
take the risk of "stepping out of her father's house."   There
is a connection that the playwrights hope the audience will
make with Electra:

> In Electra Speaks we attempt to name this universal

silence and to give voice to women. The woman in
the audience experiences her own silence, herself,
as she witnesses Electra's life and death struggle
to speak. Her speaking takes her towards separation and survival. (pp. 224-25)

When Electra steps center stage to deliver her monologue, the audience becomes aware of the rules society imposes upon women and how women express themselves. A
text note says that Electra is a character who uses the third
person to speak about herself, "about an Electra in the audience, about all women in the audience" (p. 244). For fifteen
minutes the audience is witness to an Electra who struggles
through the difficulty of expressing, not what everyone expects
her to say, but what she wants to say. While the monologue
is being delivered, the actress is embodying a range of emotions. Some of Electra's lines and their emotional content
include:

(yearn-   she knows she is not a speaker
ing)   but she has something she wants to say (p. 244)

(hope-   she's starting
ful)   she is stammering...
            and she's saying it (pp. 244-45)

            she's looking very angry
            very very angry
            but she's really sad (p. 246)

(plea   she's trying to speak for herself
for   she can't speak for herself
empathy)   she's speaking in voices ...
            she's trying to hold her own (p. 251)

Electra does manage to talk and when she does so the audience
sees a woman-identified woman.
       This play operates on an emotional level that is perhaps
stronger than the rational basis of the drama. The women accuse
the men of injustice, of moral weakness, of selfishness, and of
universal violence toward women. These claims stir up the indignation and the anger of the audience. What right do men have
to commit such barbarous injury? Who should women be denied
the right to express their own feelings and desires? As the audience ponders such questions, their emotions, aroused by the
stories, help persuade them to reject the patriarchy in favor of
a woman-identified society.
       The last play to be analyzed in this chapter portrays the

concept of the ultimate woman-identidied woman, for A Late
Snow is about lesbians. After Jane Chambers rewrote the play
(Originally it was a screenplay) in 1974, it opened at Playwrights
Horizon for a successful run.[18] After it was published in William
Hoffman's Gay Plays in 1979, lesbian theatre groups were quick
to produce the play.[19] One of the reasons for the popularity of
A Late Snow may be the fact that it is one of the first lesbian
plays to be made readily available for production.

The setting for the play is a cabin which is used by
the main character, Ellie, as a weekend retreat from city
living. For various reasons, all the characters end up at
the cabin, and all are forced, as the result of an unexpected
spring snowfall, to spend the night. Each character has a
connection to Ellie. As the action unfolds, the status of
each relationship is revealed.

The story line is simple: we witness Ellie's love life.
During the course of the play, Ellie faces the fact that her
current affair with Quincey, a former student, is coming to
a close. Enter Margo, a writer, who becomes Ellie's new
lover by the end of the play. The action is complicated by
the fact that Ellie's former lover, Pat, is present and knows
what is happening between Ellie and the other two women.
The story is really a romance, but instead of men and women,
the lovers are all women.

The playwright's primary form of proof is ethos, or
the presentation of credible characters. The women appeal
to lesbians because they are gay, but these characters appeal
to a straight audience as well. They are ordinary people,
with middle-class ideals and occupations. The intent is to
show that lesbians are people, too, and ought to have the
right to live as freely and fully as heterosexual women.

Quincey is the spokesperson for lesbian rights. She
believes that Ellie is wrong to keep their relationship "in the
closet" and advocates a more relaxed attitude toward lesbians.
During the course of the evening's conversation, Quincey talks
about the possibility for change:

> Somebody has to make change happen. Somebody
> who believes in the goodness of themselves, of
> what they are. (p. 306)

Quincey implies that the person who reveals herself as a
lesbian must be confident and ready to face the consequences
from a society conditioned by hate and fear of those who are
different. Ellie rejects Quincey's notions because of her own
years of experience. She has a job as a college professor
to consider, and admitting a lesbian preference could cost

her the job. As much as Ellie would like to be in the open,
she knows the negative consequences of revealing herself.
     In act II, a new character is introduced. This is
Peggy, Ellie's college roommate from many years before.
We find out that Peggy and Ellie were lovers, briefly, but
that Peggy opted for a conventional marriage. Now, with
her marriage on the rocks, Peggy seeks out Ellie to talk
about herself. Ellie discovers that Peggy has a friend named
Wanda, but Peggy refuses to admit what her real feelings
for Wanda are, nor will she acknowledge her affair with
Ellie. In the end, Peggy goes back to her husband and
children. When Ellie asks her about Wanda, Peggy replies,
"Wanda is my friend. That's all. That's the way it's going
to stay. I can't deal with it, Ellie. It takes courage: a
kind I haven't got" (p. 332). Peggy is unwilling to struggle
with her inner feelings, and rejects the ideal of the woman-
identified woman.
     At the end of the play, Ellie and Margo are left dis-
cussing plans for their new life together:

> Margo: How would that look, our living together?
>
> Ellie: Do you care?
>
> Margo: No.
>
> Ellie: Neither do I. I'm tired of living a half-
>   life.
>
> Margo: So am I. (p. 334)

The audience is left with the sparks of a new romance, and
the idea of a woman-identified woman who is no longer fear-
ful of letting others know her identity. Ellie decides to risk
the truth of her lesbianism with the hope of living a fuller,
more honest life.
     A review of the rhetorical strategies used in the plays
in this category indicates that the playwrights have relied
heavily on emotional proof to convince the audience to accept
the notion of a woman-identified woman. The journey of self-
discovery involved shame, as Calliope portrayed in the "Name
Your Shame" skit; confusion, such as Toni's confusion over
the appropriate image of a woman; indignation and anger,
demonstrated by the women of the House of Atreus; and fear
by all of the female characters who hesitate to face their own
identity and proclaim themselves as women.
     Many of these emotions are transformed into their
opposites as the women work through their identity crises.

At the close of the plays, characters such as Toni, Abigail, Ellie, and Electra come to terms with themselves and change the locus of their identity from others' expectations to their own expectations. In this respect, these characters have made a change from the position that Simone de Beauvoir called the "Other" to the central position of the "Self." With the establishment of a positive identity, it is indicated that the future for the characters in these plays will be more autonomous and fulfilling. And in several plays, such as Make Up by Mother Nature, Love Song for an Amazon, and Electra Speaks, the audience is shown that sisterhood results from women bonding together. These three plays also tell the audience that not only can women take the primary position in society, but society itself can become matriarchal.

While emotional proof dominates, there is still some indication of rational argument, including an instance of what Aristotle calls a "non-artistic" means of proof.[20] This is the use of testimony, which the female patient used to prove the doctor's guilt in Make Up by Mother Nature. In Focus on Me!, an incentive in the form of another character is used to provide Toni with a reason for becoming a woman-identified woman. The Web makes use of a series of maxims which the main character considered as she pondered her own behavior. And in Electra Speaks, a reinterpretation of a myth argues that the outward appearance of events is not the result of honest motivation.

Two plays, Love Song for an Amazon and A Late Snow, rely exclusively on the credibility of characters to prove the desirability of becoming a woman-identified woman. In both plays, either all or some of the characters (Rose, Aisha, and Quincey) were already in a woman-identified state and did not pass through a period of discovery and transition like the other characters.

NOTES

1. Simone de Beauvoir, The Second Sex, trans. H. M. Parshley (New York: Vintage Books, 1952).

2. Ibid., p. xviii.

3. Radicalesbians, "The Woman-Identified Woman," in Out of the Closets: Voices of Gay Liberation, ed. Karla Jay and Allen Young (New York: Douglas Book Corp., 1972) pp. 176-77.

4. Ibid., p. 172.

5. Written response to author's general questionnaire
    received from Sharon Wood for Calliope Feminist
    Theatre, December, 1981. Analysis of Make Up
    by Mother Nature based on script excerpts, a play
    description, and program notes received from
    Calliope, May 1982.

6. Program note from a performance of Make Up by
    Mother Nature, Calliope Feminist Theatre, Gideon
    Wells Jr. High School, Glastonbury, CT, 26 Feb-
    ruary, 1982.

7. Martha Boesing, Love Song for an Amazon, Minne-
    apolis, 1976. Unpublished manuscript received from
    Boesing, May 1982. Quoted passage from Preface,
    n.p. All further references to this work appear in
    the text.

8. Thanks go out to Rosemary Curb of Rollins College
    for bringing this technique to this author's attention
    in her unpublished manuscript entitled "Mounting
    Anger into Power: Alienation and Channeled Anger
    in Women's Theater." Manuscript received from
    Curb, April 1982.

9. Bobbi Ausubel, Focus on Me!, Boston 1974. Un-
    published manuscript received from Ausubel, March
    1982. All further references to this work appear
    in the text.

10. Lane Cooper, trans., The Rhetoric of Aristotle
    (Englewood Cliffs, N.J.: Prentice-Hall, 1932),
    p. 168.

11. Martha Boesing, The Web, Minneapolis, 1981. Un-
    published manuscript received from Boesing, May
    1982. All further references to this work appear
    in the text.

12. The appeal to a broader audience that The Web
    has is evident from the fact that the play was se-
    lected for production by an outside professional the-
    atre. Prior to its première on October 5, 1982
    at Trinity Square Repertory Theatre in Providence,
    RI, The Web had only been performed as a staged
    reading by At the Foot of the Mountain.

13. Cooper, op.cit., p. 150.

14. In Dinah Leavitt's Feminist Theatre Groups (Jeffer-
    son, NC: McFarland, 1980), there is a description
    of female vs. male theatre that At the Foot of the
    Mountain uses in theatre workshops. Some of the
    "matriarchal values" of feminist theatre include
    emotion, emergence, cycles, fluidity, and multi-
    orgasms. Leavitt says, "ATFM is attempting to
    develop these female traits through its work"
    (p. 68). The Web seems to be a good example of
    ATFM's efforts to create feminist/matriarchal theatre
    as opposed to male/patriarchal theatre.

15. The American Heritage Dictionary (New York: Dell,
    1969), p. 130.

16. Clare Coss, Sondra Segal, and Roberta Sklar, "The
    Daughters Cycle: Electra Speaks," Union Seminary
    Quarterly Review, 35, Nos. 3 and 4 (1980), pp.
    223-53. This article contains extensive excerpts
    from Electra Speaks and is the major source for
    the analysis of the play. All further references in
    the text are from this article.

17. Aristotle calls this a topos of paradox, in which
    "men approve one thing openly, and another in their
    secret thoughts. In public they make a great show
    of praising what is just and noble; but inwardly they
    prefer what is to their own advantage" (Cooper, p.
    167). In this play we see a refutation of what out-
    wardly appears to be deeds for the good of Greece.
    In reality they are deeds to keep the patriarchy in
    power at the expense of women.

18. Background information on the play was provided
    by William Hoffman in the Introduction to his an-
    thology Gay Plays: The First Collection (New York:
    Avon Books, 1979). A Late Snow appears on pp.
    281-335. All further references in the text are
    from this source.

19. Emily Sisley cites eight lesbian theatre groups that
    have produced the play. There are probably more
    that could be added to the list. See "Notes on
    Lesbian Theatre," The Drama Review, 25, No. 1
    (1981), pp. 52-53.

20. Cooper, op.cit., pp. 82-84.

The last six plays to be analyzed concern the perceptions of feminist theatre groups about women in the context of the family. Since the family is the primary form of organization in society, feminist playwrights are interested in the roles and relationships a woman encounters in an institution that is central to her life.

Traditionally, women characters appearing in American drama have been defined by the domestic role they play. Carol Billman says in her article, "Women and the Family in American Drama," that female characters "have been unceremoniously but inextricably tied to the home and the family." Furthermore, she contends that "we find females who, although they may in some instances question the seemingly unbreakable ties between woman and her place in the home, do accept them."[1]

The women in the feminist theatre groups could hardly be expected to perform plays with this traditional perspective. Indeed, all the plays in this chapter confront society's expectations of the typical wife and mother. The female characters of the feminist plays, more often than not, reject the bonds of domestic service in the context of the traditional marriage. If there is a central idea running through the six plays in this category, it is to urge the women in the audience to reconsider the roles they perform within the family. Marriage, motherhood, wife abuse, and the socialization of family members through language are the topics discussed in the dramas of the feminist groups. Like the plays in Chapter Four, the majority of the plays here are aimed at a female audience.

The first two plays present a strong argument against the institution of marriage. Joan Holden's The Independent Female (or, A Man Has His Pride) was first performed by The San Francisco Mime Troupe in 1970.[2] Although the Mime Troupe is certainly not a feminist group, the play was written by a feminist member of the troupe, performed before San Francisco area feminists, and first published in a

feminist journal. Enough women in the women's movement
have been exposed to the play for it to be considered feminist
drama in the context of this study.

The play, a one-act melodrama, opens with the innocent young heroine named Gloria already engaged to a junior
executive named John Heartright. The conflict of the play
centers around John's expectations of Gloria once she becomes
his wife. John wants Gloria to give up her secretarial job
in order to devote her entire life to maintaining the household and a family. Gloria's wish to remain employed is rejected by John and her own mother. Gloria's mother tells
her that the basic difference between men and women is that
men have a strong sense of pride and it would be Gloria's
job to help John maintain his pride (p. 123).

A second problem that Gloria faces is whether or not
to participate in the office strike her coworker is organizing.
The coworker is a feminist named Sarah Bullitt, who believes
that women should demand their rights--"equal work with men,
equal work by men, equal pay for equal work" (p. 125). Not
only does Sarah persuade Gloria to help organize the strike;
she also argues against Gloria's impending marriage to John.
She tells Gloria, "If you want your independence you'll have
to sacrifice your chains. Very soon now you'll have to make
a choice" (p. 125).

The arguments against marriage are presented as forensic discourse. Sarah accuses men of hypocrisy in the roles
they play, while John defends the traditional role functions:

> John: You girls were made for the lighter work--
>   washing, cooking, raising children.
>
> Sarah: And you for the heavy stuff eight hours a
>   day. Why men are so strong, they get
>   paid for work we do; promoted for ideas
>   we have; they get their names on books we
>   write.
>
> John: This bitterness is what makes your life dif-
>   ficult. If men have privileges--it's because
>   we've earned them. After all, males are
>   responsible for every major achievement of
>   civilization.
>
> Sarah: War, waste, competition, pollution, inflation....
>
> Gloria: What have we done?

> John: Take Gloria, forever prattling about the way
> things should be; she needs me to stand be-
> tween herself and reality. Why aren't you
> girls content to be what we need? Compe-
> tent secretaries ... thrifty housewives....
> (p. 124)

In the next scene Sarah advances a similar argument,
while Gloria defends the traditional female role.

> Sarah: How can you marry that swine?
>
> Gloria: We're engaged! And you can just save
> your breath--I've accepted my role as a
> woman.
>
> Sarah: To gratify, amuse, cushion, flatter, and
> serve.
>
> Gloria: We should let men be boss, since it means
> so much to them.
>
> Sarah: To be seen as a piece of meat by every
> man who walks by?
>
> Gloria: That's the price we pay for being attractive.
>
> Sarah: You're preparing to spend your days as
> personal property. You'll end up with no
> life. (p. 124)

After a series of arguments such as this, Sarah is able to
convince Gloria to reject marriage and to make a commitment
to help liberate the female office workers.
    When 100,000 women in the city go on strike, negotia-
tions begin between the capitalists (men) and the women.
Sarah pulls out a .357 Magnum and starts making revolution-
ary demands for arms and control of the city. John shoots
Sarah, but Gloria grabs the gun and triumphantly vows to
"turn your [men's] prison homes, and your frozen minds,
and your whole profit, progress, power monster male system
over." She concludes by saying, "And when we all have our
independence, then we can all have our pride" (p. 131). When
Gloria leaves the stage at the end of the play (still toting the
.357 Magnum!), a barker appears and asks the audience,
"Does the implacable rebellious spirit of independent females
portend this society's ultimate collapse? Young ladies and

gentlemen, the future lies in your hands" (p. 131).
The melodramatic form serves as an effective structure for presenting an argument based on credibility.[3] The
characters are reduced to ideal types which makes it very
easy for the audience to identify the personality and moral
conduct of the characters. The rigid moral distinctions that
accompany characters are a form of ethos used by the playwright to prove a point. The heroines (Gloria, Sarah) and the
villain (John) evoke the appropriate emotions in the audience.
Michael Booth makes the point that "melodrama appeals to
the most elemental feelings of the audience and to their instinctive desires for a better world."[4] Certainly, The Independent Female arouses a desire for equality (at home and
in the workplace) in the female audience members.
    Holden's play is not without logical proof. In the
argument between Sarah and John, Sarah tries to show that
men use women to achieve their own selfish goals rather
than bettering the world for everyone's benefit.[5] In the
argument between Sarah and Gloria, Sarah outlines the negative consequences of acting out a traditional role. She tells
Gloria that women are dehumanized and reduced to sexual
objects. Other logical proof used by Sarah includes a comparison of salaries--"our average wage is 50 percent of men's"
(p. 128)--and quotations from nineteenth-century feminist Lucy
Stone.
    The Independent Female offers the audience two alter-
natives to the problem of inequality. Women are urged to
reject marriage entirely if they want to be "independent"
(free) human beings. Women are also urged to strike in
order to gain equality as workers.
    The next play concentrates strictly on the institution
of marriage. As in The Independent Female, the message is
to reject marriage, but in this play we see the consequences
of marriage itself, instead of predictions that keep a woman
from going through with the marriage. River Journal, by
Martha Boesing, was first performed by At the Foot of the
Mountain in 1975.[6] The play is structured like a Brechtian
drama. There are six characters: Ann (the protagonist),
Myles (her husband), Ann's father, Vera (one of Ann's alter-
egos), Carla (Ann's other alter ego), and Snake (a mother
goddess who comments on the action). The play opens with
a wedding ceremony and ends with Ann leaving the marriage.
The scenes in between are episodic and often begin or end
with commentary from Snake. Boesing makes use of the
personality fragmentation technique to expose a woman's
archetypal behavior patterns in marriage.[7] Ann is a new
wife who wishes to reclaim herself as a human being. Vera

is the flirty, sexual part of Ann. Carla is the helpmate who
keeps homelife in order. Each of the alter egos wears a
mask to characterize her role.

The play depicts the marriage of Myles and Ann from
Ann's point of view. Throughout the play, Ann struggles to
fulfill her role(s) in the relationship in the way that society
expects. Through Carla, we see a depiction of the mother-
ing behaviors a wife performs--making meals, sweeping floors,
settling quarrels, catering to Myles' needs. Vera performs
all of the sexual behaviors to make Myles happy. The rapid
succession of scenes is punctuated by songs that comment on
the action and by readings from a journal that Ann is keeping
The journal entries are bizarre descriptions of Ann's dreams
and inner thoughts. They give clues to her emotional state,
which is quickly degenerating into insanity as a result of the
marriage. Ann is filled with sadness over the loss of her
autonomy and with anger toward the roles that Carla and Vera
represent. The audience should take pity on Ann and her
situation.

In the Preface to the play, Boesing writes, "River
Journal deals with the ritual patterns of marriage in a male-
dominated society in which ownership is power" (p. 32). In
the play, the character who clearly represents this point is
Ann's father. In one scene he is talking to Myles about the
difficulties of marriage. When Myles asks him why he married Ann's mother, he responds:

> Sometimes it passes through my mind that the
> reason I married Ann's mother was that I was
> better than she and could prove a necessary and
> important component to her growth, could make
> her over, in a manner of speaking, save her from
> the trials of an otherwise unenlightened and pedes-
> trian existence; and hence garner the satisfaction
> of having contributed to the bettering of the human
> race. (p. 66)

Dad's speech is certainly enough to rankle the sensibility of
the audience toward the institution of marriage, which is,
of course, what it is designed to do. In spite of Dad's
words, it should be noted that neither he nor Myles are portrayed as evil characters. Both of them have good intentions.
They are genuinely concerned about Ann's mental and physical
health. They may behave conventionally, but it is not because
they are the enemy. Instead, their behavior is a result of
ignorance and socialization:

What is a man to do?
Misguided and misinformed,
He throws himself on the waters of life,
And surrenders his dreams to the storm!
(p. 60)

The cause of Ann's problems is shifted onto "the
system" rather than specific people. This seems to indicate
that we need to get rid of both the whole cultural institution
of ownership by marriage and the roles that accompany the
custom. At the end of the play, Ann burns the masks that
represent Vera and Carla and tells Myles she must leave the
marriage to "move into the center of [her] own dreams"
(p. 77). The cast sings to the audience:

The question is laid out
For each of us to ask:
Whether to hold on
or to drop the mask. (p. 78)

Like a typical Brechtian play, River Journal serves
as an example to the audience to warn them against a social
ill. The "insanity of marriage" is depicted by the traditional
behaviors which the female characters perform. Guided by
the songs that serve as transitions between scenes, the audience is eventually advised to choose either freedom or a role
that restricts a person's well-being. Ann's rejection of her
role in marriage indicates to the audience the choice that the
playwright favors.
Central to the life experience of most women is motherhood. Many feminist theatre groups have written plays on the
topic, and it continues to be an important issue that feminists
wish to understand better. The author of one of the motherhood plays that is examined here remarked that she thought
motherhood would be the single most important issue for
feminist drama to explore in the next few years:

The important radical position, I think, for women
in this culture, has to be motherhood. That's the
issue women have to address. Most of the women
in this country are mothers. [8]

                    Bobbi Ausubel
                    Caravan Theatre

Ausubel's play, Tell Me a Riddle, is an adaptation of
Tillie Olsen's short story by the same title. [9] The central
character is an old woman named Eva. She is an extremely

bitter person who constantly argues with her husband. As
the reasons for her bitterness are revealed, it becomes apparent that the author is presenting the audience with the
negative aspects of motherhood. The drama is another example of epideictic rhetoric, in which the negative conditions
of the role are emphasized. Our pity for Eva is increased
when it becomes known that she is dying of cancer.

The dialogue among family members gives clues to
the past. Eva bore seven children, one of whom died. She
raised them in circumstances of dire poverty. She begged
for soup bones and kindling. She mended clothes until they
were threadbare. In the middle of winter she took the children to sleep at the train station because there was no heat
in the house. Her life was governed by cleaning, cooking,
washing, and tending the children. Her husband David never
made enough money, nor was he ever at home.

The family's harsh life seems to Eva a sequel to the
life she experienced as a young girl. She was brought up
in a Russian village, where she experienced the horror of
the Revolution. She was thrown into prison for being a Jew,
and upon her release married David and emigrated to the
United States. Eva has left behind both her country and her
religion, which taught prayers that said, "In Paradise, woman,
you will be the footstool of your husband" (act I, p. 14).

After "moving to the rhythms of others" for over sixty
years, Eva wants to be left alone to enjoy her Chekhov books
and Beethoven records. Most important, she wants silence.
But David will not let her alone. He wants to sell the house
and move into a planned retirement community. They argue
violently about selling the house, but Eva will not give in.
With bitterness she says, "Vinegar he poured on me all my
life. I am well marinated. How can I be honey now?" (act
I, p. 4).

When David finds out that Eva is stricken with cancer,
he insists on taking her to visit all the children. Eva witnesses her own daughters "drowning in motherhood" and is
unable to enjoy her grandchildren: "Unnatural grandmother,
not able to make myself hold a baby. Oh, please, do not
ask me. I cannot" (act I, p. 18).

After an operation, Eva is taken to Los Angeles to
recuperate near the ocean. She retreats further into herself and her music. The only one who understands Eva is
a grandchild named Jeannie, a nurse. She comforts Eva as
best she can, but David and Eva's own children cannot understand her. Eva dies a tortured and lonely death.

The author has relied on emotional proof to show that
motherhood is an undesirable role. Eva is a pitiful character

who has endured great pain and suffering in order to provide
for her children. The audience is moved to sympathy and
indignation that any woman should exist solely to care for others.
The depiction of Eva's torture is a highly personal and psychological example of one woman's experience with motherhood. Revealing the interior feelings of the character to the audience
is a technique that was used by the playwrights who wrote
dramas concerning the woman-identified woman. Boesing
also used it in River Journal so that the audience could see
the psychological damage brought on by the demands of marriage.

Bobbi Ausubel's (and Tillie Olsen's) portrayal of motherhood shows the audience that the reverence often bestowed
upon the role is not necessarily accepted by those who function as mothers. Aristotle says that the ends of epideictic
discourse are honor and dishonor.10 Ausubel has shown us,
through Eva's interpretation, how motherhood might be viewed
as something less than honorable, even though Eva herself
is not dishonorable.

In contrast to Tell Me a Riddle, Martha Boesing's
The Story of a Mother offers a different point of view.11
Boesing's play is a ritual that celebrates all aspects of moth-
erhood.12 Like River Journal, The Story of a Mother ex-
poses negative archetypal behavior patterns, but it also extols
the positive. By witnessing and participating in the enactment of the behavior patterns, the audience communally exor-
cises the negative aspects of motherhood while celebrating
the positive. This play can also be considered epideictic,
but its purpose is to honor a role that many women perform
in their lifetime, rather than to dishonor it.

In Chapter Two, The Story of a Mother was described
as a play that is divided into many segments. Each segment
focuses on a particular aspect of motherhood: initiation rites,
birthing, mothers comforting daughters, separation of the
mother and the adult daughter, etc. Each segment is a magni-
fication of a condition of motherhood. After the behavior pattern of each condition is enacted by the theatre company, a
structured ritual is conducted in which audience members give
testimony from their lives, recalling the behaviors of their
own mothers.

The last ritual serves as a celebration. The actresses give bread to the audience members and say something
like, "Let the mother within feed the child within" (p. 49).
A song about the bonding of mothers and daughters is sung
as the bread is passed around. As the play draws to a
close, the actresses and audience members renew their identity through their mothers. All stand and introduce them-

selves in this way: "I am Jody, daughter of Ann."

The primary form of proof is the testimony offered
by the audience members themselves. In this situation, each
person in the audience functions as a rhetor, providing testimony from personal experience. The testimony is accompanied
by much emotion. The mother-daughter relationship is a complex one in which the participants feel a great deal but rarely verbalize those feelings. The use of audience participation
allows for a form of self-persuasion that results in a positive view toward motherhood.[13]

The next play focuses, once again, on the negative
side of marriage. Internal Injury, by the Rhode Island Feminist Theatre, is a play about domestic violence.[14] As in the
previous play, the primary means of persuasion is testimony.
However, the testimony in Internal Injury comes from three
women, Helen, Peg and Jo, who are victims of serious physical abuse. They serve as witnesses to a crime committed
by men who are not punished by society for their criminal
behavior.

The stage is divided into three sections, which represent the homes of each of the three central characters. The
set and the appearance of the characters indicate that the
women are from a cross section of socioeconomic groups.
This is designed to emphasize that wife beating is prevalent
in all social strata. Each woman states her case in a series
of monologues describing past action by the husband. After
a round of monologues (and sometimes interaction among the
women), the three characters use choral recitations as transitions into the next set of monologues and scenes. Each
round reveals a different aspect of the problem. The men
never appear in the drama, nor do we witness any actual
abuse, but the message is clear: wife beating is still a
common practice in our society, and its pervasiveness must
be exposed to the general public if the problem is going to
be solved.

The play is structured somewhat like a forensic argument. The men are accused of the crime:

> Peg: My nose was bleeding. He kicked me in the
> stomach then. I was five months pregnant.
> (p. 8)

> Helen: He ... he hit me, he hit me and hit me and
> hit me. (p. 11)

The statistical magnitude of the problem is expressed to the
audience in one of Helen's speeches:

There are 23 million women who, like I was, are
beaten by their husbands. That's one wife in four.
Think about it. One in four. (p. 4)

We find out the reasons the women remain in the
abusive situation for so long: "It's for the kids." "I'm afraid
of being alone." "He has a right to get angry." "There is
nowhere you can go" (p. 4). Many women deny both to themselves and hospital officials that the husband has inflicted
injury. The emotional bond between the husband and wife is
sometimes all the wife can sustain the relationship with:

Jo: I think Kris really needs me. (p. 4)

Peg: I gotta go back to what I know, what I love.
       I love Bill, we can work it out. (pp. 39-40)

The police are often unwilling to answer calls involv-
ing domestic violence, and they are declared guilty for not
aiding the victims of the crime. Helen recalls:

And I'll never forget what the police said to me.
"Don't call us again tonight, lady, we have a lot
of other calls to attend to." You have to be dead;
that's what they need to act. (p. 40)

The end of forensic argument is usually a judgment
of guilt or innocence in relation to the accused. In this
play, the accused (men) are not present, so the playwrights
offer the victims several possible actions in the face of the
problem. First, a woman can continue to deny the abuse
and hope that everything works out. Jo is the character
who denies her problem. Second, a woman can go to a
shelter where she will receive counseling and child care.
Professionals at the shelter can help a woman start a new
life on her own or get back with her husband. Third, a
woman can walk out on her husband and get a divorce. Helen
is the character who selects the third option, and we see
that this is the solution advocated by RIFT. Peg opts for
the shelter, but cannot stay long enough to get the help she
needs. Several days later an obituary appears in the paper:

Margaret Hollis. March 8, 1978. In her home
of injuries from falling down stairs. (p. 43)

It is horrifying to discover not only that Peg was killed, but
that her death has been covered up by her husband and any

medical examiner who might have suspected that she was a
victim of abuse.   The audience fears that Jo's denial of her
own situation may lead her down the same path.
     The emotional arguments in this play are very strong.
The audience is outraged at the injustice of the crime and
pities the victims.   When this author saw Internal Injury performed, however, the evidence that affected the audience most
was the statistics.[15]   Helen's speech occurred very early in
the play, yet the audience members who stayed for discussion
remembered the numbers.   Many people were astounded that
23 million women in this country are victims of beatings.
The magnitude of the problem is clearly expressed in these
numbers and may be the single most important kind of proof
in the entire play.   And it may be RIFT's intention to use
statistics as a way of shocking the audience into taking action
to solve the problem.
     The last play to be analyzed in this chapter concerns
language and its relationship to role behavior.   In her play,
American King's English for Queens, Megan Terry has selected
the family unit as the context for exploring the question, "Do
you think like you talk or talk like you think?"[16]   Through
the dialogue that punctuates a family's interaction, the audience
is shown that language helps to shape sex roles, leads to expectations of others based on sex, and determines social control.   The play is different from all the other plays in this
chapter because the focus is on a family rather than a single
female character.   The family unit is viewed as a stifling
institution that affects all its members, and not just the
woman who functions in the role of wife or mother.
     The play is divided into two acts and each act focuses
on different actions to demonstrate the thesis of the play.
However, the idea of language affecting the status of people
is portrayed more through a dramatization of stereotypical
behavior than through use of language, as the title of the play
would suggest.   In the first act, the audience is witness to the
homelife of the Connell family.   This gives the audience an
overall view of how children are socialized through language
and role models, and how adults maintain learned roles.   In
the second act, the children socialize a snipe, a female character who is a completely unsocialized humanoid animal, into
the family.   The snipe is a focus for the way in which any
being is socialized according to its sex.   In both acts, the
language that is used by the characters is directly linked to
their sex roles.
     The conditioning of sex-role behavior in children is
demonstrated in a scene in which three of the children are
playing a board game.   When the girls ask Doug to play, he

says he's not interested in "a girl's game," but ends up joining in anyway. His sisters run through a list of occupations
appropriate to men: "Boys can be airline stewards, actors,
teachers, and principals" (p. 24). When Jaimie and Kate
insist that stewardesses are fliers, Doug refutes them with
"not in this game. They're waitresses. Just like at Pizza
Hut" (p. 25). When Doug draws a "personality card" that
says his makeup is too sloppy to be an airline hostess or
model, the girls laugh hysterically. Doug tries to take control of the game by threatening his sisters, but they just
continue to laugh at him.
    In another scene, Dad is training Doug to be a man.
He shows him how to stand properly and to hitch up his pants.
He gives Doug some necessary advice:

> Men don't have to snarl to get respect. You do
> not beat up on your sisters. A man protects his
> sisters, his wife, and his mother. (p. 38)

This scene emphasizes the cultural custom we have in which
the male parent trains the male children to follow certain
behavioral patterns, and the female parent trains the female
children. The male behaviors described in the passage above
include superiority and dominance over females, albeit in the
guise of protection for them.
    The mother in this play is portrayed as an oppressed
servant to husband and children. In every scene in which
she appears, she is either cooking a meal, dusting furniture,
or performing some other household chore. She has a tendency to daydream romantically about the past and often won-
ders aloud who she really is. As she stirs the stew she says
to herself, "Who are you? I'm Mrs. Daniel Connell, and
I'm making veal stew" (p. 18). She identifies herself as an
extension of her husband and as a domestic servant.
    The father, on the other hand, constantly talks about
money, his office, stock options, etc. When his personal
secretary is transferred out of the office, he comes home
in an uproar. He angrily demands, "Let me have a drink
and read the paper and take my nap before dinner" (p. 52).
His wife obediently responds by getting the drink. All of
the concerns and behaviors of Dad, Mom, and the children
are specific to society's expectations of the roles they hold.
    In act II, the children go on a snipe hunt and capture
one. The snipe, which they discover is a female, is socialized into the family. The three daughters decide to teach
her to speak the language of humans, but they agree that
they'll "have to think of a way we can teach her to talk with-

out making her feel that being a girl is not as good as being
a boy" (p. 63). In the end, the snipe has been transformed
into something like Miss America. The question of proper
identity is emphasized in the snipe's declaration to the audience that "this family helped me to make the transition from
animal kind to mankind.... Womankind? Humankind? Our
Kind?" (p. 3).

After a performance of the play, the Omaha Magic
Theatre had "humanists" lead discussions with the audience.[17]
The humanists were professors of English, philosophy, history, linguistics, and communication who served as advisors
during the research period of the play. Using a worksheet
prepared by Megan Terry, the humanists and the audience
explored "the effects of the English language on the status of
women in America" (p. 82).

The rhetorical impact of the play is actually derived
from audience participation during the discussion period. Furthermore, the discussion question posed is related more to
feminist concerns than the action of the play. The subordinate
position of women that is maintained through language is not
really emphasized as much as it should be if this play is
directed toward women's problems, as the theatre group
claims. Perhaps the goal of the play is simply to make
people aware of the effects of language so that audience members will be more sensitive to their own choice of words.

Feminist theatre groups have taken a keen interest in
the role that women play in the family. Most of the plays
in this analysis have pointed toward the negative aspects of
the family, often urging women to reject marriage and the
trappings of family life. If motherhood is indeed a topic for
future feminist drama, as Bobbi Ausubel has predicted, then
perhaps audiences will be offered a more thorough understanding of the role and its relationship to society. If we were to
judge the outlook of the nuclear family based on the plays in
this chapter, then it might be easy to predict the demise of
the family as we know it today. These are angry plays, for
the most part, and take a radical feminist position. While
Gloria Steinem is telling viewers of the Merv Griffin Show
that "equal parenthood will be the issue of the 1980's," most
of these feminist theatre groups are telling audiences that
women should reject motherhood and marriage altogether![18]

The last three chapters have devoted considerable space
to the analysis of twenty feminist dramas. The plays were
grouped according to the central idea that guided the words
and actions of the characters. In Chapter Three, the plays
classified as "sexual politics" depicted the power of patriarchy
and urged women to reject it. In Chapter Four, the plays

analyzed explored the ways in which women identify and define
themselves, a category called "the woman-identified woman."
The female audience was urged to define themselves based on
female characteristics, and to bond together as woman-identified women. In this chapter, the plays classified as dealing
with "family roles and relationships" have depicted the role
of the woman in the family. The depictions were overwhelmingly, though not universally, negative and most urged women
to reject marriage and motherhood as those institutions now
function in society.

The messages of the feminist theatre groups reveal
several common characteristics. The use of emotional appeal
is dominant. The female characters in the plays express
deep anger, and in some instances, hatred toward the male
characters, but at the same time they fear the power and
control men have over them. Plays such as The End of War
and Internal Injury are especially poignant because they show
how men physically and sexually abuse women as a means of
control. The plays that concern women and their journey toward a new identification demonstrate how women fear and
distrust themselves and their own potential for accomplishment.

The characters in many of these plays are portrayed
as ideal moral types in order to prove a point. Even though
The Independent Female is the only true melodrama, many
of the other plays contain characters who function in a similar way. Less than half of the plays contain well-developed
characters. The audience is often presented with archetypes
rather than realistic personalities. The playwrights have a
tendency to pit the men against the women to demonstrate
how women are victimized in unjust situations by malevolent
men.

For the most part, the logical proof in these plays
consists of examples and testimony. The testimony comes
from female witnesses who are characters in the play, or
from the personal experience of the audience members. The
plays call for audience participation both during a performance
of a drama (The Story of a Mother) and after performance in
the form of discussion (How to Make a Woman, Paper Weight,
American King's English for Queens, to name a few). This
testimony is highly personal, but it is considered by many
to be representative of the experience of most women. Other
logical proof centers around the use of paradox--using role
reversal (The Johnnie Show) and a reinterpretation of events
(Electra Speaks) to point out the feminist perspective of the
situation. And in one play (Internal Injury), the authors use
statistics to prove the extent of domestic violence in American
households.

Overwhelmingly, the plays function as deliberative discourse. The audience is usually advised to reject anything that has to do with men, but very often, a concrete solution or suggestion of immediate action is not provided. The audience members leave the theatre knowing what the playwrights favor, but also realize that each woman (or man) must make an individual decision for action based on her/his own situation. The deliberative impact usually overrides the forensic arguments that provide an internal structure for the plays. When the plays contain male and female characters there is often debate over particular issues. The arguments clearly delineate the female vs. the male point of view, and in all cases, it is the female perspective that is advocated by the theatre groups. In the plays in which advice is not offered, it is still apparent that the playwrights are calling for approval or disapproval of the situations depicted in the drama.

The patterns of argument that emerge from the feminist theatre dramas coincide with the patterns evident in other types of women's liberation rhetoric. Karlyn Kohrs Campbell describes the stylistic rhetorical features of feminist discourse as follows:

> Women's liberation is characterized by rhetorical interactions that emphasize affective proofs and personal testimony, participation and dialogue, self-revelation and self-criticism, the goal of autonomous decision making through self-persuasion, and the strategic use of techniques for "violating the reality structure."[19]

The feminist dramas analyzed in this study employ all the devices described by Campbell. It is the firm contention of this author that, based on the evidence, feminist drama is rhetoric, and that theoretically, the drama can and does persuade audiences by using the same kind of strategies as other types of women's liberation rhetoric.

NOTES

1. Carol Billman, "Women and the Family in American Drama," The Arizona Quarterly, 36 (1980), p. 35.

2. Joan Holden, The Independent Female (or, A Man Has His Pride), in Notes from the Third Year, ed.

Anne Koedt and Shulamith Firestone (New York: n.p., 1971), pp. 120-131. All further references to this work appear in the text.

3. This strategy was discussed earlier in Chapter Three.

4. Michael Booth, English Melodrama (London: Herbert Jenkins, 1965), p. 38.

5. This is the same strategy used by the characters in Electra Speaks. See Chapter Four, p. 69

6. Martha Boesing, River Journal, Minneapolis, 1975. Manuscript received from Boesing, May 1982. All further references to this work appear in the text. Note: the manuscript is paginated; pp. 32-78.

7. This technique was used in the plays of the woman-identified woman. See Chapter Four, note 8.

8. Personal interview with Bobbi Ausubel in New Haven, CT, 31 March 1982.

9. Bobbi Ausubel, Tell Me a Riddle, Boston, 1977. Unpublished manuscript received from Ausubel, March 1982. All further references to this work appear in the text. Ausubel's play is based on the title story in Tillie Olsen's Tell Me a Riddle (London: Faber and Faber, 1964).

10. Lane Cooper, trans., The Rhetoric of Aristotle (Englewood Cliffs, N.J.: Prentice-Hall, 1932), p. 18.

11. Martha Boesing, "The Story of a Mother: A Ritual Drama," in Women In American Theatre, ed. Helen Chinoy and Linda Jenkins (New York: Crown, 1981), pp. 44-50. Boesing's play concentrates on the mother-daughter relationship.

12. See Chapter Two, note 31 for Boesing's definition of ritual.

13. For further discussion of this point see Chapter Six, pp. 104-105.

14. Rhode Island Feminist Theatre, Internal Injury,

Providence, 1979. Unpublished manuscript received
from RIFT, December 1981. All further references
to this work appear in the text.

15. RIFT, Internal Injury, dir. Janet Buchwald, Eagen
Auditorium, University of Scranton, Scranton, PA,
21 March 1982. The 23 million figure is difficult
to corroborate because meaningful statistics on wife
abuse are not readily available. A 1978 Newsweek
article contained the figure 28 million, and Donna
Moore wrote in the Introduction to her book, Battered Women, "Nationwide, the FBI estimates that
wife abuse occurs three times as frequently as
sexual assault, and they further estimate that it is
reported less than 10% of the time. This would
mean that wife abuse occurs approximately every
18 seconds somewhere in the United States" (p. 14).
It appears that RIFT does have a reasonable figure.
See Jerrold Footlick and Elaine Sciolino, "Wives
Who Batter Back," Newsweek, 30 January 1978,
p. 54, and Donna Moore, ed., Battered Women
(Beverly Hills: Sage Publications, 1979), pp. 12-15.

16. Megan Terry, American King's English for Queens
(Omaha: Omaha Magic Theatre Press, 1978). All
further references to this work appear in the text.

17. The humanists led discussion during the original run
of the play, March-April 1978. Their contributions
are noted in the script. Also of interest is a tran-
script of one discussion held at Creighton University
in Omaha, printed as an appendix to the script, pp.
82-102. Source cited above.

18. The Merv Griffin Show, 30 June 1982. Gloria
Steinem appeared as a guest during the tenth an-
niversary celebration of Ms. magazine.

19. Karlyn Kohrs Campbell, "The Rhetoric of Women's
Liberation: An Oxymoron," The Quarterly Journal
of Speech 59 (1973), p. 83. Use of role reversal
would be the obvious example of the way in which
theatre groups "violate the reality structure."
Campbell's examination of liberation rhetoric includes
books, essays, discourse, and the content/style of
consciouness-raising.

Chapter Six
FEMINIST THEATRE AS BELIEF-BOLSTERING PERSUASION

This chapter examines the idea that the persuasive effects of feminist drama are geared more toward bolstering the beliefs of audience members (and the members of the theatre group) than changing those beliefs. The tenet was established in Chapter Two that feminist theatre is a multi-locational rhetorical process. This chapter extends that notion by saying not only that persuasion occurs at many points in the communication process, but that at several points the persuasion is of a very specific kind; that is, it is belief-bolstering.

The theoretical framework for the discussion of belief-bolstering effects is based on the work of William McGuire and Edwin Black.[1] While a social scientist and a rhetorical theorist certainly adhere to entirely different methodologies, the results of their investigations are surprisingly compatible. Both of them offer justification for the psychological effects of feminist drama on audience members and theatre group members.

McGuire offers an explanation for the way in which audiences rationally react to persuasive discourse. His theory is based on a series of experiments which he conducted in the early 1960's as part of a body of research in the general area of inducing resistance to counterpersuasion. In this paradigm, a person's resistance is conferred by defensive messages which he/she receives in a pretreatment condition. The defensive messages contain arguments on a given issue which the person can then employ in the future to resist any kind of persuasive attempt on that particular issue.

In the case of feminist theatre, the arguments presented in the drama provide a defense for audience members (and actors) who might be challenged to defend their beliefs on feminist concerns. Since the evidence points toward the fact that both feminist theatre group members and the majority of the audience are already feminists, the argument will be advanced that the drama serves to strengthen or solidify

feminist beliefs that already exist in the minds of those participating in the theatre event.

This strengthening process is similar to the condition
McGuire describes as "supportive defense." The term "supportive defense" is defined as a nonthreatening message which
contains arguments in support of the issue.[2] For example,
the group of plays analyzed in Chapter Three under the heading "sexual politics" provides the audience with general arguments in support of the existence and consequences of a sexual
politics ideology. Should the audience members (or actors)
be challenged at a later time to prove that patriarchy oppress-
es women, they will have arguments to draw on from the
drama showing how patriarchy dehumanizes women, perpetu-
ates stereotypes, and aids the oppression of women through
rape and abortion laws, etc.

McGuire's notion of supportive defense is based on the
assumption that audiences respond on the basis of logical
decision-making, and that they will subsequently defend a
position using logical argument. The analysis of feminist
drama in Chapters Three through Five, however, indicates
that the arguments used by feminist theatre groups are primarily emotional, and that logic definitely holds a position
of secondary importance. We must account for the emotional
factors at work in the belief-bolstering process. Black's
theory of rhetorical criticism allows us to do so.

The genre of women's liberation rhetoric, of which
feminist drama is a part, is a distinct genre that is characterized by emotional and moral suasion.[3] It is a rhetoric
of extremism and is similar to religious revival rhetoric,
rhetoric of the New Left, abolitionist rhetoric, and rhetoric
of the Right. Black describes this genre as:

> ...one in which the evocation of an emotional ex-
> perience in the audience induces belief in the sit-
> uation to which the emotion is appropriate instead
> of following as a consequence of belief in the sit-
> uation[4]

What this passage predicts when applied to feminist theatre
is that feminist audiences already hold certain beliefs that
are strongly tied to emotional responses. The perceived
oppression of women implies moral judgments that stem
from a universal notion of justice and injustice. These
moral judgments involve volatile emotions. The theatre
groups, by providing verisimilar situations in the drama,
evoke similar emotional responses in the audience. The
response is not a judgment to believe or disbelieve; it is

a response of greater commitment to a conviction already
held. Black explains this idea further:

> The most plausible and reliable source of informa-
> tion we have is our own experience.... Therefore
> we have a strong proclivity for validating our feel-
> ings by accepting appropriate beliefs. The power
> of exhortation lies, first, in its capacity for evok-
> ing intense emotion, and second, in its capacity for
> legitimatizing the emotional experience with appro-
> priate convictions. [5]

The emotional response to feminist drama results in commitment to feminist convictions. The committed audience will
return to the rational arguments in a feminist play for further validation of their convictions. This is where McGuire's
theory ties into Black's. The logical arguments not only
offer the audience a rational justification for an emotional
commitment, but they also offer the audience a weapon for
intelligently defending their position against the opposition.
    The remainder of this chapter provides an illustration
of the commitment and belief-bolstering processes as they
occur in the feminist theatre phenomenon. The focus of the
discussion is on the audience, but the actors also receive
some attention.
    There is little doubt that the women who belong to feminists
theatre groups are feminists themselves. The fact was pointed
out in the first few pages of Chapter Two that most of the women
who founded their own theatres are both theatre artists and feminists. One of the goals of many feminist theatres is to combine
the art of theatre with the politics of feminism:

> The impetus for founding our theatre group was to
> combine interests in feminism and theatre and to
> make feminist political statements. [6]
>
> Calliope Feminist Theatre
>
> RIFT's main goal over the eight years of its exist-
> ence has been to produce original full-length drama,
> inspired by feminist perspectives on the world. [7]
>
> Rhode Island Feminist Theatre

The extensive analysis of plays in Chapters Three, Four,
and Five is a further demonstration of the theatre groups'
goal to present a feminist message to the audience.
    Examination of the names of feminist theatre groups

reveals interesting implications for what might be expected
from a feminist performance. Of the one hundred twelve
women's theatre groups listed in Women in American Theatre,
thirteen have the word "feminist" somewhere in the title, and
twenty-eight use a derivative of "woman" to indicate that it
is a women's group. [8] The subjective reactions that potential
audience members make to those two words probably determines who in the community will support the theatre. At
the same time, the use of the words "feminist" and "woman"
in the name may be purposely used by the theatre group to
project a particular image to the community. Women's theatre groups who wish to appeal to the general public rather
than to cater only to a feminist contingent are quick to point
out that the name will often predetermine the makeup of the
audience:

> We are a commercial organization for we feel that
> only thru [sic] commercial theatre will the largest
> audiences be reached. If feminist is associated
> with your name, the only audience that attends are
> people sympathetic to your cause--they do not need
> to be educated. [9]

Eccentric Circles Theatre

The Eccentric Circles Theatre raises an interesting
point. If feminist theatre is used as a channel to change the
public's attitudes towards women, then perhaps a commercial
enterprise would be the appropriate vehicle for change. If
feminist theatre is a channel used by feminists to reach other
women in the liberation movement, then perhaps the community
needs to know that feminism is associated with the theatre
group. The data collected for this study indicate that, by
and large, the target audience of most feminist theatre groups
appears to be women. [10] Several groups testify to this fact:

> Our prime audience has been members of the local
> women's community and we are constantly expanding. [11]

Calliope Feminist Theatre

> In the period 1975-77, when the women's movement
> needed strength, the entire company (both men and
> women) decided to direct their efforts to women's
> issues--at that time it was necessary to talk to
> women. [12]

Omaha Magic Theatre

> Our audience is very broad--and seems to cross all kinds of lines. Our aim is to reach women.[13]
>
> Sondra Segal
> Women's Experimental Theatre

> Our primary audience is women. But I wish that more men would participate.[14]
>
> Sharon Dailey
> Indiana State University
> Listener's Theatre

Roberta Sklar has suggested that women be allowed to have their own space away from men to create and transmit women's experiences through the theatrical form:

> We ask for the same space [as male playwrights writing about men]. To look at what goes on between women in the world. To not be clobbered with the fear of lesbianism because it's an irrelevant question. To looking at [sic] the relationship between mothers and daughters, and sisters, and friends, and lovers. To not have to suddenly send up a red flag and say, "but if you leave the men out, what will the women do?" We want the time and space, however long that may be, and it might be as many centuries as the men have left us out. We want that without feeling that we're hurting somebody else, whether we owe someone else. But, we must think about the men while we do our work.[15]

Sklar's comments went on to indicate that the absence of men pertains not only to actors and the content of the drama, but to the audience as well.

This author's own attendance at feminist theatre performances supports the idea that audiences are primarily made up of women. On the average, ninety percent of the audience was women, and the men in attendance were almost always in the company of women.[16] In New Haven, Connecticut, this author observed that many of the women who were at a performance by the Rhode Island Feminist Theatre (from Providence) were also at a performance by the Theatre of Light and Shadow (based in New Haven). The two performances were four months apart and in two different auditoriums. Members of the Theatre of Light and Shadow verified the fact that the women's community in New Haven comprises a regular part of their audience and supports other feminist theatre groups, like RIFT, whose members visit on occasion.[17]

Historically, it seems that feminist theatre began as communication among women, often to the complete exclusion of men. Charlotte Rea's article, "Women For Women, " in The Drama Review, begins with the statement:

> The theatre done by these groups is aimed at a specialized audience and often is performed exclusively for that audience--women. Almost all of the women's theatre groups reserve at least one of their performances for women only, and most prefer to play only for women, even when they admit men.[18]

Rea's article covered some of the very early feminist theatre groups including It's All Right To Be Woman, Womanrite Theatre, and The New York Feminist Theatre Troupe. While the majority of groups today still target their drama toward women, the necessity of excluding men from performances is not as apparent. Sharon Dailey's wish that "more men would participate" is indicative of the liberal attitude that women's theatre should extend to humankind rather than excluding any segment of society.

In fact, the question of leaving men out of women's theatre was a major concern at the recent Women in Theatre Conference held in New Haven. One of the conclusions drawn from the discussion was that even if men are not physically present at a theatre event, their impact is still felt. Roberta Sklar acknowledged this when she said, "We must think about the men while we do our work. "

A special consideration arises in discussion of lesbian theatre groups. The presence of lesbian groups strongly supports the assumption that much of women's theatre exists for other women. For example, Rosemary Curb's "Catalog of Feminist Theatre" documents the target audience of two lesbian groups. Red Dyke Theatre of Atlanta, she says, aims "to entertain lesbians and celebrate their sexuality, not to educate straight people about lesbians and gay issues."[19] Most of the performances of Medusa's Revenge, a lesbian theatre in New York, she continues, are attended by lesbians and feminists.[20] Dinah Leavitt's case study of the Lavender Cellar Theatre in Minneapolis shows that the original members tried twice to form a unified group that could provide a voice for the Minneapolis lesbian community. The group specifically sought a gay audience and performed at the Lesbian Resource Center.[21]

The lesbian community often aligns itself with the local feminist theatre, whether or not the theatre group is lesbian.

Some feminist theatres, who wish to remain anonymous, have indicated a certain amount of pressure from their lesbian following who want the theatre to perform more overtly lesbian drama. One feminist theatre group member expressed real shock at the prevalence of lesbian demand from the audience attending the First Women's Theatre Festival in Boston in 1980, at which her theatre performed.

> We really got a tremendous amount of pressure
> from people [lesbians] up there because they felt
> we were not dealing with the issues at all.   They
> were very radical.   Very strongly separatist.   It
> was a shocking experience for me.

This anonymous comment is just one of several received during data collection for this project.   The point to be made is that there is a real demand by the lesbian community for theatre that speaks to lesbians only.   When lesbian drama is not available, lesbians will attend other feminist performances, searching for intellectual and/or emotional identification and entertainment value.   One of the implications of the pressure exerted by lesbians on feminist theatres is that, in this instance, rhetor and auditor exchange places.   Lesbians hold an extreme left position in the women's movement.   It appears that it may be their intent to get feminist theatre groups who hold a more moderate position to make a commitment to a more radical one.   Once the theatre groups perform drama that speaks primarily to lesbians, they narrow both the issues they could discuss, and the audience they would attract. [22] This notion is one that is certainly worth further investigation.

The evidence offered up to this point establishes two inportant points that tie into the theory of belief-bolstering. First, the rhetors are feminists whose intent is to influence audiences composed of women.   Second, the audiences who attend feminist theatre productions are feminists themselves, who are probably predisposed in their reactions to the plays. We need to illustrate the probable predispositions further in order to confirm that feminist drama does, indeed, result in firmer commitment to convictions.

Feminist theatre is essentially political, but the politics of the theatre groups are so similar to the beliefs and opinions of the audience members that overt political change is not readily apparent as a goal of feminist theatres.   Rather, the drama functions, as Michael Kirby has pointed out in his article "On Political Theatre," to "give emotional and intellectual support to those who already agree with its position." [23]

Some of the feminist groups are reluctant to admit that they
play to sympathetic audiences, but the evidence points toward
the reality outlined by Eric Bentley:

> Much drama that makes controversial points, re-
> lies, without ever admitting it, on the audience's
> prior agreement.[24]

This researcher made a brief attempt to investigate
the notion that feminist theatre audiences agree with the beliefs expressed by the theatre groups prior to witnessing a
performance. An audience-reaction questionnaire was dis-
tributed at a performance by the Rhode Island Feminist Theatre (RIFT) in Scranton, Pennsylvania.[25] Twelve people out
of the sixty-six in attendance returned the questionnaire. Out
of the twelve, nine (including a male respondent) said they
considered themselves feminists, two said they weren't sure,
and one male respondent said no, he was not a feminist. Out
of the twelve, nine said they actively participated in the wom-
en's movement. Two of the nine were the respondents who
weren't sure whether they were feminists!
     The play RIFT performed was Internal Injury, a drama
about domestic violence. Of the twelve respondents, eleven
said they were already in accord with the play's message and
that the play did, indeed, reinforce beliefs they already had
about the problem. The performance of Internal Injury was
put on as a benefit for the Women's Resource Center (WRC)
of Scranton. Most of the people in the audience were volun-
teers at the center, or were guests of people affiliated with
the center. One of the goals of WRC is to raise money to
build a shelter for battered women in Scranton. Most, if
not all, of the people in the audience were already aware of
the prevalence of domestic violence. Most had direct experience working with abused women and knew the causes of the
problem. So while Internal Injury may have had definite persuasive power, the persuasion that was effected in Scranton
was not mind-changing. Rather, the play reinforced what
most of the audience already knew.
     A similar reaction occurred in New Haven at a perfor-
mance of RIFT's Paper Weight,[26] a play about women office
workers and the discrimination they experience on the job.
Eighty out of the ninety audience members were women,
mostly white, middle-class, in their mid-twenties. Forty-
three women and two men remained after the show for a
half-hour discussion. The general comment was that audience members could identify with certain characters. Even
during the performance and intermission there were laughs

of recognition or comments indicating that audience members were seeing their own lives portrayed on the stage. The people in real life who controlled the economic destiny of clerks were not in the audience that evening. Rather office workers, much like the characters in the play, comprised the audience, and their own beliefs about job discrimination and powerlessness were being reinforced.

Other feminist theatre groups draw an audience that returns again and again to see performances. Carol Asmus of Calliope Feminist Theatre says, "We see the same people and always some more."[27] The principles of dissonance theory lead to certain logical conclusions about the loyal following that many feminist theatre groups have. Dissonance theory says that when a person encounters beliefs that oppose the beliefs already held, that person will seek out messages similar to those held in order to resolve the dissonance.[28] By seeking reinforcement from similar messages, a person is able to maintain psychological consonance which has been validated from outside sources. Feminists who regularly attend feminist theatre performances will come away from the experience with renewed validation of the feminist ideological position and will be capable of resolving any dissonance that may be created by the opposition. Feminist audience members specifically choose to attend a feminist theatre event because they feel comfortable and reinforced by the ideology that accompanies the entertainment.

Since the media do not regularly cover feminist theatre events, the loyal audience must seek out information about upcoming performances from alternative sources.[29] Since feminist performances are generally irregular and often in a different location each time, simply finding out about events requires a real effort on the part of the audience. The audience must have a strong desire to see a feminist performance if they go to such trouble to find out about it.

Chapter Two mentioned the common practice of audience participation during a feminist theatre performance. Participation--whether on the part of the actor or audience member--is similar to making a public commitment to the beliefs expressed in the drama. The act itself can be a very strong form of psychological bolstering. Not only does a woman reinforce her own thoughts and feelings on the topic being presented, but she also demonstrates to her peer group her willingness to support a feminist point of view. Black makes the point that participation is a "nonrhetorical" strategy, but that it can be an important part of the overall transaction:

One of the many nonrhetorical forces at work in
cases of spoken exhortation may be the condition
of the auditor as a member of an audience. In
such a case, the auditor's private emotions pass
into a public domain. He will have accepted beliefs
sanctioned by the acceptance of others, and this
certainly will sustain him in his new belief.[30]

The Story of a Mother, by Martha Boesing in collaboration with members of At the Foot of the Mountain, offers
an interesting case of public commitment during performance.[31]
The drama is composed of a series of ritualized moments in
which actors and audience members express their emotions
about their experiences with their mothers. During the run
of the play, many of the audience members returned again
and again, bringing with them their own mothers and daughters,
or friends. Very few men attended performances.

The ritual moments allowed the audience members to
express words and actions that had occurred between themselves and their mothers as they were growing up. Martha
Boesing reports that the idea of using ceremony to express
emotion was extremely successful. By bringing loved ones
into the drama as a focus for exploring one's own feelings,
many of the audience members were able to realize, "My
mother loves me." The participation allowed the audience
to experience a series of fundamental emotions in a public
context. The rituals led people from anger to fear to dis-
tress to a feeling of abandonment and, finally, to understanding. By the end of the play, the audience, as a group, had
reached a point of renewal, knowing that they could forgive
(or be forgiven for) all that had transpired, and that everything between mother and daughter was all right.

The public commitment to a positive mother-daughter
relationship is unusual, and it seems significant that a theatre can provide the context for recognition of deep emotions
that have developed since childhood. While many women
have privately pondered the negative ties between themselves
and their mothers (aided by books such as Nancy Friday's
My Mother/My Self), few women have been able to work pub-
licly through negativism to arrive at positive experiences.
At the Foot of the Mountain has provided such a unique experience for its audience.

How can a two-hour theatre experience successfully
solve private problems by expressing public solutions? Many
people spend weeks in encounter groups or attend one-to-one
meetings with a professional counselor trying to work through
difficult relationships in their lives, so why should theatre

presume to offer anything more effective? One of the reasons
might be the "safe" environment offered by the theatre experience.
Martha Boesing describes the ritual approach to drama:

> We choose ritual instances from cultural life that
> are ceremonial, that have a spiritual base. The
> attachment to spirit implies that we are working
> with the emotions and vulnerabilities of each par-
> ticipant [both actors and audience members]. The
> audience is first a witness to the revelations of
> the actors, and then participants themselves. The
> audience feels safe relating their own emotions
> because the actors have just done so. A safe en-
> vironment for sharing is created. [32]

Belief-bolstering is very apparent in the work of At the Foot
of the Mountain. "Ours is a theatre of recognition, not rev-
elation, " says Boesing. The environment provided by ATFM
allows the audience to move from "a state of psychological
stalemate to a state of empowerment." The goal of moving
an audience to a state of empowerment is aptly described by
Eric Bentley in his essay "The Theatre of Commitment."
Bentley describes the ideal audience as those "who may be
vaguely sympathetic to the cause preached but are a little
sluggish and sleepy about it. They may assent but they are
not really committed, and the purpose of the Drama of
Commitment is not to be for commitment but to get people
to commit themselves." [33] Perhaps At the Foot of the Mountain's use of ritual drama is a key to moving "sluggish" audience
members to a real commitment.

Other theatres provide a recognition process for their
audiences. For example, Pro Femina in Washington, DC
uses women's experiences as a basis for the drama they
present in order to generate a sense of commonality with
the female audience. [34] By theatrically showing people the
choices made by theatre group members and where those
choices lead, the audience can make connections in their
own lives with what is happening on the stage.

Some of the key words that describe the effects that
feminist theatres have on their audiences are recognition,
connection, identification, and realization. All of these
words do not describe abrupt changes; rather they imply that
there is a bridge between the action presented on stage and
the life experiences of the audience members. The message
that is presented in the form of a drama is a message that
reinforces or clarifies what the audience members have already experienced.

The audience members are not the only ones to be
affected by a feminist theatre production. What about the
actors? What does happen to the theatre group members,
who have an ongoing exposure to feminist ideas? Janet
Brown's statement quoted in Chapter Two (p. 24) acknowledges the rhetorical impact of playwriting and performing on
those involved in these actions. She also says the impact
may be different from the effect on audience members; however, she does not go beyond mere acknowledgement. It is
important to consider the effects of feminist theatre on writers
and actors, for these are the women who are participating
in the women's movement as authors of feminist statements.

What persuasive effects occur as the women participate in the group as communicators? Theatre group members
engage in research when writing and rehearsing a new play,
which provides a possibility for change in other directions.
But participating members are all feminists, so they should
also be reinforced by their public statements on feminism.
Is this belief-bolstering or persuasion that results in attitude
change? More than likely it is both.

Says Susan Chast, a member of the Theatre of Light
and Shadow, "Within the company too there are people who
say, 'Thank you for making this change in my life.' It's
not just the audience, it's within the group. Every time
I'm involved in rehearsal it's powerful for me."35 Two kinds
of impact are evident in this statement. First, there is an
overt change through the act of joining and becoming part of
the group. Perhaps the member becomes a full-fledged feminist or makes a long-lasting commitment to feminist art as
political expression. Second, there is a renewal of commitment, or an intensification of belief, each time the member
is involved in performance. The political philosophy of
feminism is intensified every time that member acts out a
drama that embodies a feminist statement. This is very
similar to the public commitment just discussed in relation
to audience participation.

For many members of feminist theatre groups, the
experience they get as members is an education in feminism.
The Rhode Island Feminist Theatre and At the Foot of the
Mountain both agree that members learn, grow, and mature
as a result of the theatre experience.36 Because of the
emphasis on feelings and emotions, many members gain significant insight into themselves as people, and more impor-
tantly, as women who are feminists. Those who stay with
a theatre group over a long period of time develop a strong
commitment to a feminist way of life. The politics and
life-styles of the theatre group members result in a very

well-defined feminist position. The stronger the commitment to feminism, the more likely it is that theatre group members close off their options for alternative politics and life-styles.[37] Since many of the theatre groups are collectives, there is a strong sense of commitment to group-accepted choices and a concomitant rejection of other choices. The longer a group stays together, the further they move from the mainstream of social life and politics.

Another aspect of feminist theatre is that often the members own a share in the theatre. Having economic autonomy in their professional lives demonstrates to the group members that it is, indeed, possible for them to accomplish their goals without answering to men. The confidence gained from this knowledge encourages the members to pursue their independence, both in their private lives and in the work they do related to the theatre. While the autonomous existence may be frugal, it is viewed by those who manage it as a positive step. Moreover, they are proud to tell others of their success. It is certainly a sign to women in their audience that autonomy is not only desirable, but attainable.

Chapter Two described the research conducted by some of the theatre groups when they prepare a new play. At this stage of the communication process there are rhetorical effects taking place that probably induce or strengthen commitment to feminist beliefs. The effects, however, are as difficult to measure here as they are in the audience participation phase of the process. Because the effects occur on an individual basis it is difficult to gauge the impact on a general level. Moreover, the involvement of members of the theatre group will vary during the research period, so that persuasive effects will not be uniform.

Nevertheless, some generalizations about the research period can be made. The earliest theatre groups spent much time participating in consciousness-raising sessions as an integral part of the development of the drama. Many of the members were exploring their individual needs and trying to define the concerns of the women's movement. The ambiguity of the situation probably resulted more in attitude change toward particular issues than in any kind of belief-bolstering.

Today, feminist theatre groups do not have to spend a great deal of time making decisions about appropriate issues-- most of them are already established. Therefore the development of a drama involves analysis of an issue from a feminist perspective more than selection of an issue. A research period now requires building an argument for the case rather than just finding out about the case. This is overtly reflected in the fact that feminist plays today are generally full-length

dramas rather than one-acts. A full-length drama allows the
theatre group to present a more developed discussion of an
issue, whereas a one-act usually does not go very far beyond
the naming or identifying of an issue for consideration by the
audience. The trend to full-length drama seems like a logical
progression in the rhetorical development of feminist drama.
The initial "naming the enemy (or issue)" is the first stage,
and is followed by rhetoric that builds off that stage. [38]
    Evidence gathered during the research period not only
adds substantial arguments to the content of the play; it also
serves as a source of ideas that may be used during the
actor-audience discussion following performance. Several
times during a discussion of the implications of Internal
Injury I heard members of the Rhode Island Feminist Theatre
referring to information gathered during the research period
as proof of the extent and consequences of domestic violence. [39]
Most of the proof centered around statistics they had gathered
but did not incorporate into the actual play. The implication
here is that the research period provided confirmation of
RIFT's original ideas about domestic violence and served as
a source of supporting material that could be drawn upon at
any time during the playwriting and performance stages. Thus,
the effects of the research period may vary according to the
way material is utilized at any given point in the communication process.
    This chapter has attempted to build a case for feminist
theatre as belief-bolstering persuasion. Using a theoretical
framework based on the work of William McGuire and Edwin
Black, we have seen that commitment to feminist convictions
is largely the result of emotion, but that logical arguments
offer a rational justification for the commitment and serve
as support when feminists encounter arguments from the opposition. The evidence offered here points toward the idea
that much of the commitment occurs in the context of group
research and public participation. As this commitment to a
feminist ideology is strengthened over time, both theatre
group members and audience members have a tendency to
reject incompatible arguments. In the next chapter we will
explore the nature of the feminist ideology that is evident in
the drama and look for a connection between the ideas in the
drama and in the women's movement.

NOTES

1. William J. McGuire, "Inducing Resistance to Per-
    suasion: Some Contemporary Approaches, " in Ad-
    vances in Experimental Social Psychology, ed.
    Leonard Berkowitz (New York: Academic Press,
    1964), I, pp. 191-229; and Edwin Black, Rhetorical
    Criticism: A Study in Method (New York: Macmillan,
    1965).

2. McGuire, op. cit., p. 202.

3. Karlyn Kohrs Campbell, "The Rhetoric of Women's
    Liberation: An Oxymoron, " The Quarterly Journal
    of Speech 59 (1973), pp. 74-86.

4. Black, op. cit., p. 118.

5. Ibid., p. 145.

6. Written response to author's general questionnaire
    received from Sharon Wood on behalf of Calliope
    Feminist Theatre, December 1981.

7. Publicity brochure for 1981-82 repertory season
    received from RIFT, September 1981.

8. Helen Chinoy and Linda Jenkins, Women in American
    Theatre (New York: Crown, 1981), pp. 343-45.

9. Written response to author's general questionnaire
    received from Rosemary Hopkins on behalf of Ec-
    centric Circles Theatre, February 1982.

10. The general target audience is all women, but it
    will become increasingly clear in this chapter that
    not all women attend feminist theatre.

11. Written response to author's general questionnaire
    received from Sharon Wood on behalf of Calliope
    Feminist Theatre, December 1981.

12. Written response to author's general questionnaire
    received from Rose Marie Whiteley on behalf of
    Omaha Magic Theatre, July 1982.

13. Written response to author's general questionnaire
    received from Sondra Segal on behalf of the Women's
    Experimental Theatre, March 1982.

14. Written response to author's general questionnaire
    received from Sharon Dailey on behalf of the Indi-
    ana State University Listener's Theatre, March 1982.

15. Roberta Sklar, "The New Women's Theatre" panel
    discussion, Women in Theatre Conference, New
    Haven, CT, 31 March 1982.

16. This percentage is based on attendance at five fem-
    inist theatre performances in the northeastern
    United States between November 1981 and May 1982.
    It may not necessarily be accurate. Pro Femina
    of Washington, DC, claims that 66 percent of its
    audience is female, while At the Foot of the Moun-
    tain in Minneapolis claims that 70 percent of its
    audience is female. Ninety percent might be too
    high when compared to data gathered by feminist
    theatres.

17. Personal interview with members of the Theatre
    of Light and Shadow in New Haven, CT, 1 April
    1982.

18. Charlotte Rea, "Women For Women," The Drama
    Review, 18 (December 1974), p. 77.

19. Rosemary Curb, "Catalog of Feminist Theatre--
    Part 2," Chrysalis, No. 2 (1979), p. 70.

20. Ibid., p. 72.

21. Dinah Leavitt, Feminist Theatre Groups (Jefferson,
    NC: McFarland and Co., 1980). See pp. 43-52
    for a summary of Lavender Cellar activities.

22. Black. op. cit., p. 162. The effect of lesbian
    pressure would be to force the theatre group to a
    "firm and increasingly well-defined position."
    Black says this "works to prohibit them [theatre
    groups] other positions that, in the course of con-
    troversy, become concomitantly firm and well de-
    fined."

23. Michael Kirby, "On Political Theatre," The Drama
     Review, 19 (June 1975), p. 135.

24. Eric Bentley, "The Pro and Con of Political Theatre,"
     in The Theatre of Commitment (New York: Atheneum,
     1967), p. 131.

25. Rhode Island Feminist Theatre, Internal Injury, dir.
     Janet Buchwald, Eagen Auditorium, University of
     Scranton, Scranton, PA, 21 March 1982.

26. Rhode Island Feminist Theatre, Paper Weight, dir.
     Janet Buchwald, Educational Center for the Arts,
     New Haven, CT 21 November 1981.

27. Kristina Goodnough, "Calliope Feminist Theatre
     Dramatizes Women's Issues," Courant, n.d., Sec.
     D, pp. 1, 10. Photocopy of article received from
     Calliope Feminist Theatre, December 1981.

28. Leon Festinger, A Theory of Cognitive Dissonance
     (Evanston, IL: Row, Peterson, 1957).

29. Lack of media coverage has always plagued feminist
     theatre, as Patti Gillespie points out in her article
     "Feminist Theatre: A Rhetorical Phenomenon,"
     The Quarterly Journal of Speech, 64 (1978), 284-85.
     Word-of-mouth and mailing lists are probably the
     most successful advertising tools available to fem-
     inist theatres.

30. Black, op. cit., p. 146.

31. See Chapter Five for an analysis of the play. The
     description of participation on the following pages
     is based on a telephone interview with Martha Boesing,
     5 September 1982.

32. Telephone interview with Martha Boesing, 5 Septem-
     ber 1982.

33. Eric Bentley, "The Theatre of Commitment," in
     The Theatre of Commitment (New York: Atheneum,
     1967), p. 226.

34. Horizons, a National Public Radio Program, WFSU-
     FM, Tallahassee, FL, 3 February 1981. Interview

with Leslie Jacobson of Pro Femina Theatre. (I
would like to thank Kathleen Banner for bringing the
program to my attention.)

35. Personal interview with members of the Theatre
     of Light and Shadow in New Haven, CT, 1 April
     1982.

36. Taped response by Sherilyn Brown on behalf of the
     Rhode Island Feminist Theatre to interview questions,
     received September 1981. Telephone interview with
     Martha Boesing, 5 September 1982.

37. This follows as an extension of Black's idea about
     argumentation described in note 22 above.

38. Brenda Hancock ("Affirmation By Negation In the
     Women's Liberation Movement, " The Quarterly
     Journal of Speech, 58 (1972), pp. 264-71), indicates
     that the first stage of women's liberation rhetoric
     was to name the enemy and, concomitantly, estab-
     lish the pro-woman argument. She says that re-
     cent feminist rhetoric "is now stressing action pro-
     grams and social change" (p. 271), which is evi-
     dence of the stages of argument in a radical move-
     ment. Much of Hancock's thesis is based on Leland
     Griffin's ("A Dramatistic Theory of the Rhetoric of
     Movements, " in Critical Responses to Kenneth Burke,
     ed. William Rueckert [Minneapolis: University of
     Minnesota Press, 1969], pp. 456-478) description
     of movement rhetoric which involves the stages of
     inception, crisis, and consummation. The inception
     stage would, in large part, be made up of rhetoric
     that negates the existing order and the people who
     represent that order. (I would like to thank Dr.
     Marilyn Young for discussing with me her ideas
     about the rhetoric of radical movements, developed
     in her seminar on the rhetoric of extremism.)

39. Rhode Island Feminist Theatre, Internal Injury,
     dir. Janet Buchwald, Eagen Auditorium, University
     of Scranton, Scranton, PA, 21 March 1982.

Chapter Seven
FEMINIST THEATRE AND THE WOMEN'S MOVEMENT

The Ideology of Feminist Drama

In 1970, Robin Morgan wrote in the Introduction to
Sisterhood Is Powerful that alternative institutions such as
women's child-care centers, halfway houses, referral services,
and feminist media were emerging in response to the demands
of a radical women's movement. Among the media named
were books, magazines, newspapers, and theatre groups.[1] It
is interesting to note that the early theatre groups were viewed
by women in the movement as instruments of communication,
capable of transmitting messages supportive of the movement
itself. Two questions are posed in this chapter in regard to
the function of feminist theatre as a communication medium
for the women's movement. First, how can the messages
of the theatre groups be classified as far as ideology is concerned? Second, are feminist theatre groups a successful
medium of communication for relaying messages of the movement to audiences?

Patti Gillespie's article, "Feminist Theatre: A Rhetorical Phenomenon," describes the content of feminist theatre
as radical.[2] Much of the analysis in Chapters Three, Four,
and Five in this study supports that point of view. But what
is meant by "radical"? Kathie Sarachild, founder of consciousness-raising (CR), defined "radical" as follows:

> It is a word that is often used to suggest extremist,
> but actually it doesn't mean that. The dictionary
> says radical means root, coming from the Latin
> word for root. And that is what we meant by call-
> ing ourselves radicals. We are interested in get-
> ting to the roots of problems in society. You might
> say we wanted to pull up weeds in the garden by
> their roots, not just pick off the leaves at the top
> to make things look good momentarily. Women's
> Liberation was started by women who considered
> themselves radical in this sense.[3]

If we agree with this definition, and if we consider that many
of the early feminist theatre groups were involved in CR techniques, then we can easily see how much of the drama has a
radical content. Sagas of hairy legs, stories about bras, dia-
tribes on rape and abortion laws are themes that indicate how
feminist theatre group members probed their problem of oppression down to its most intimate level.

Morgan also boldly stated, "Women's liberation is the
first radical movement to base its politics--in fact, create
its politics--out of concrete personal experiences. We've
learned that those experiences are not our private hang-ups.
They are shared by every woman, and are therefore political."[4]
If we agree with Robin Morgan's statement about the content
of feminist politics and measure the content of feminist drama
by it, then certainly we can say that feminist theatre groups
are structuring radical messages, for the content of almost
all feminist drama comes out of the personal lives of the
theatre group members. Feminist theatre groups write their
own drama, and the reality they depict comes from their own
experience. Consciousness-raising techniques have provided
a means for theatre group members to probe down to the
roots of their oppressive experiences, which they then portrayed on the stage in the form of problem plays.

Chapter Two traced the development of feminist theatre
groups in part to the New Left movement. The women who
departed from the New Left were radical in their ideology,
and those who found their way into feminist theatre groups
continued to follow a leftist line of thinking. Only the cause
was new: women's liberation.

The plays analyzed in Chapter Three are a prime example of "getting to the roots" of the problem of female oppression in American society. Taken as a whole, the plays
offer a fairly complex investigation of the phenomenon known
as sexual politics. Beginning with Persephones Return, a
play about how men came into power in the first place, through
Taking It Off, a play about sexually oriented power struggles,
to The End of War and But What Have You Done For Me
Lately?, two plays that depict the oppression of women through
rape and unjust abortion laws, the audience is clearly offered
a radical point of view about feminist problems.

It is only the last play in the analysis, Paper Weight,
that proposes to solve a problem through an agency of the
conventional system. At the end of that play, women office
workers are drawing up a petition to seek representation on
policy-making boards at their place of work. Not only is a
petition a very middle-of-the-road solution, but the problem
it attempts to solve--discrimination against women in the 80%

--is something that has concerned groups like NOW and other organizations that seek change through existing mechanisms.*
     It is interesting to note that Paper Weight is the most recent of the plays in the group. It might also be noted that the Rhode Island Feminist Theatre (RIFT) is the collective author of both Taking It Off and Paper Weight. The latter was written six years after the more "radical" play, Taking It Off, was produced. Is the divergence in perspective an indication of the ideological direction that feminist theatres are moving in? Not necessarily. In an interview, RIFT member Sherilyn Brown said, "Not only do we not have one ideology, but I would never want to see us have just one. I think we have a pretty broad spectrum of feminist perspectives within the theatre, and as hard as that can be sometimes, it's really important to making good theatre."[5] In the same interview Brown also said, "I would say that our drama for the general public definitely makes radical statements. From a strict political definition, yes, we are radical, we depart from the status quo." So what is apparent in the history of this particular theatre group is that drama can consistently make radical statements, even if the approach softens over time.
     Of the fifteen theatre groups who responded to the general questionnaire sent out for this study, two-thirds said that their plays made statements that could be called radical.
     When one considers the fact that feminist theatres do not operate within the boundaries of commercial theatre, then a number of connotations immediately arise, including "radical," "experimental," "political," "confrontational," etc. Feminist theatre as a theatre form can trace its origin not only to the New Left Movement but also to the Off-Off Broadway theatre of the 1960's. Part of this lineage is inherently radical on social, political and economic levels.
     Furthermore, plays by feminist theatre groups are almost never produced by other theatre groups, whether feminist or otherwise. There is an independent set of women playwrights (often with a feminist vision) who write for more mainstream audiences. This set includes Adrienne Kennedy, Wendy Wasserstein, Corrine Jacker, Marsha Norman, Honor Moore, Jane Chambers, Tina Howe, Eve Merriam, Susan Griffin, Maria Irene Fornes, and other familiar names whose

---

*Women in the 80% refers to those women who work in low-paying, dead-end type jobs such as clerical, service, and factory jobs. These women constitute 80% of the female labor force.

work is recognized on a different artistic level than the work
coming out of the feminist theatre groups. [6] The drama written by individual playwrights who have no connections with a
particular feminist theatre group is intended as a very different kind of statement than the drama associated with a group
of individuals who write, produce, and act in that drama.
What are some of the "statements" that are made by
the feminist theatre groups, and how do these ideas corre-
late with the major ideas put forth by participants in the
radical women's movement?

One of the basic arguments of radical feminists is that
men are the enemies of women because they are directly responsible for the oppression of women. The New York Radical Feminists clearly stated this in the manifesto which was
drawn up at their first meeting in 1969:

> As radical feminists we recognize that we are en-
> gaged in a power struggle with men, and that the
> agent of our oppression is man insofar as he iden-
> tifies with and carries out the supremacy privileges
> of the male role. [7]

The concept of man as enemy led to a separatist ideology,
in which feminists advocated the establishment of exclusive
female relationships and social institutions. [8] The woman-
identified woman (discussed in Chapter Four) is a corollary
idea, along with the pro-woman argument which essentially
says that women have positive characteristics that should be
recognized for their worth. [9]

The plays in Chapter Three certainly depict man as
the enemy. The sexual politics theme that runs throughout
the plays indicates the kind of power struggle between men
and women that is described in the passage above. It is
especially apparent in the plays by the Rhode Island Feminist
Theatre. Taking If Off and The Johnnie Show clearly pit the
men against the women. In Persephones Return, the audience
is shown how power was taken from women in the first place,
and how women can now reject patriarchy for a more androgynous society. The character portrayals emphasize the
negative characteristics of men. In The End of War, the
men are rapists and torturers. They are rapists again in
Persephones Return. In Babes in the Bighouse, men are
shown as brutal punishers sanctioned by the State. In But
What Have You Done For Me Lately?, a woman actually
names man as the enemy. [10] Of all the plays analyzed in
Chapter Three, this one is the most forthright in blaming
men for the oppression of women. The vocabulary is blatant

and the target of the woman's hatred is obvious.

The plays in Chapter Four focus more on the separatist concept that is the result of recognizing man as the enemy. Although we do see male characters in The Web and Make Up by Mother Nature, there is not much in the way of direct confrontation between men and women. Dr. Ben Dover is the obvious enemy in Make Up, but in the other plays men are the understood rather than the outright agents of oppression. In Love Song for an Amazon, there is mention of "they" and "barbarians," which we assume are men, but the focus of the play is on the relationship between two women. In Electra Speaks, we know that Electra steps out of her father's house because she chooses to reject the oppression imposed by a patriarchal family, but there are no male characters in the play who represent the patriarchy. The authors of the play say that "there is a feminist confrontation with Being" at the center of Electra Speaks, indicating a focus on indentifying what it is to be female.[11] This is definitely a play that falls under the woman-identified woman or the pro-woman line of argument. Likewise, Focus on Me! and A Late Snow both describe the positive characteristics of women and women's capability to function as autonomous human beings.

The radical feminists in the women's movement have felt very strongly that the nuclear family is a manifestation of oppression and that with the dissolution of the family unit women would be free to establish themselves as people first, and as mothers or wives second.[12] In four of the plays analyzed in Chapter Five the audience is shown a rejection of marriage and/or motherhood by the female protagonist. In River Journal, Ann leaves her husband, Myles, when she realizes she cannot fulfill the roles that are expected in a marriage. In The Independent female, Gloria not only rejects her fiancé, John; she also becomes the leader of a strike movement by women office workers. In the end she chooses her "sisters" and the struggle for independence over marriage and servitude to John. In Tell Me a Riddle, Eva rejects her roles as mother, wife, servant, and grandmother through psychological withdrawal. She does not physically leave her husband and family, but she takes on an outward silence that masks her interior life--which is a series of recollections from childhood. The audience is not shown an alternative to the status quo, but the oppression of women in marriage is very evident. In Internal Injury, the audience is shown the choices that three women make in response to marriages filled with violence. Helen leaves her husband and establishes her own, independent life. Peg chooses to return home and is inadvertently murdered by her

husband. Jo, who has been beaten by her husband, but hasn't
decided what to do about it, is the last person the audience
sees on stage. A judgment about Jo's future is left up to
the audience.

In each play in which the female character rejects
marriage, the family, or motherhood, it is indicated that
her future will include support from other women, whether
it is from a consciousness-raising group, a strike group,
or a matriarchal society. This foreshadowing of the future
is strongly pro-woman. The audience is told that rejecting
men or denouncing them as the enemy can only lead to the
formation of sisterhood and the recognition of female traits
as positive qualities rather than as handicaps.

Clearly the majority of plays in this study do represent a radical point of view, and many issues "discussed" in
the plays closely parallel the major issues that have been
raised by radical feminists. However, there is some evidence that the most recent plays by feminist theatre groups
are not as radical in approach as some of the older ones,
and that overt feminist radicalism may be giving way to new
philosophical directions.

Some feminist theatre groups are now exploring human
problems rather than continuing to focus on women's problems.
The impending danger of nuclear destruction has probably in-
fluenced the content of the latest drama produced by feminist
groups more than any other national or global event. This
is significant when one considers that in June of 1982 the
Equal Rights Amendment was defeated in the United States.
This is not to say that the approach of all feminist theatre
groups is less radical, or that the problems of women are
being forsaken in favor of humanistic politics, but the trend
is a possibility.

Betty Friedan recently said, " I think women's most
basic issues now converge on men's, the basic issues of war
and peace and economic survival, of quality of life for young
and old. "[13] There is evidence among the theatre groups
that this convergence of issues is very real. In the 1982
revival of The End of War, playwright Karen Malpede dedicated the production "to all the world's peoples currently
engaged in the effort to disarm." Her dedication came from
the realization "that there will be no art, no creativity, no
birth, no love, no life, if nations continue to manufacture and
to own nuclear weapons."[14] Also in 1982, At the Foot of the
Mountain presented a new play entitled Ashes, Ashes, We All
Fall Down. One theme of the play is nuclear war. At the
end of the play, audience members light candles for their
own loved ones, then all the candles are blown out as a

symbol of impending nuclear destruction. Playwright Martha Boesing commented, "It [the play] says, 'You are responsible. You are involved, whether you like it or not. This is your issue and your children's.'"[15] In a telephone conversation with this writer, Boesing added, "We did the nuclear piece because we felt it was urgent."

The Omaha Magic Theatre has been categorized frequently as a feminist theatre, even though the theatre does not make a feminist claim. From 1975 to 1977, Omaha Magic Theatre did specifically address women's issues, and two of the plays from that period are analyzed in this study (Babes in the Bighouse and American King's English for Queens). In response to a questionnaire, a spokeswoman for the group said:

> Today, we feel the need to isolate women (to address them as a group) does not exist and our plays are directed toward humanistic themes--topics of human interest, i.e., Goona Goona, our recent piece about all forms of violence in the family and the piece we are working on now, Kegger, about youth and alcohol.[16]

The preoccupation with addressing topics from a humanistic perspective is even apparent in American King's English for Queens. As described in Chapter Five, the play deals with sexism in language, but rather than using a setting of direct confrontation between men and women, playwright Megan Terry selected the family as a means of demonstrating the theme. This approach allowed the audience to see the problems of language and role on a broader scale. Furthermore, the discussions following the play were led by "academic humanists" who probed the implications of the play with audience members. Omaha Magic Theatre has used the humanists on more than one occasion as a teaching/learning tool for the benefit of both audience and theatre group members.

In summary, the content of the plays analyzed in this study confirm the notion that feminist drama is radical, and that the statements of the drama can be aligned with the radical feminists' ideology in the women's movement. There is evidence that the recent issues discussed in the drama are related to human concerns rather than women's concerns, but that the line of argument is still leftist.

The Success of Feminist Theatre As a Communication Medium

    The analysis of any rhetorical situation must include
some evaluation of the impact of the message on an audience.
Chapters Two and Six discussed the persuasive effects of
feminist drama, and the potential theoretical impact of drama
when it functions as a message. But one question remains
unanswered when one considers feminist theatre as a communication medium of the women's movement, and that is,
how successful is theatre when compared to other communication forms that feminists have used to spread the ideas of
the movement?
    The answer seems elusive and ambiguous if one con-
siders impact in terms of sheer numbers. It is difficult to
tell how many people have seen a feminist theatre production
since the first ones were offered in the late 1960's. During
the six-year lifespan of It's All Right To Be Woman Theatre,
founder Sue Perlgut estimates that fifteen to twenty thousand
people saw the group perform.[17] Dinah Leavitt reports that
At the Foot of the Mountain is seen by over five thousand
people a year.[18] Since the theatre's founding in 1974, it can
be estimated then that about forty-three thousand people have
witnessed and/or participated in the drama by At the Foot of
the Mountain. However, the reader should interpret these
numbers with caution because the total figures surely include
people who come back repeatedly to see performances.
    Typically the seating capacity at a feminist perform-
ance is small. Usually, one hundred people is considered
a good turnout. At a conference, a feminist theatre may
by lucky enough to perform for five hundred to two thousand
people. A recent newsletter for a women's theatre festival
estimated that there are over six hundred feminist theatres
functioning in the United States.[19] Formal listings of feminist
theatres include the names of just over one hundred groups.
It is doubtful that six hundred feminist theatres do indeed
exist. But, if the number were that large, and if each
theatre did reach several thousand people a year, then we
could estimate that about two million people a year in the
United States witness a feminist theatre production. (And
this is certainly a generous estimate!)
    The numerical impact of feminist theatre seems min-
imal when compared to print media. The Feminine Mystique
alone has sold over two million copies since its first print-
ing in 1963. Ms. magazine has a monthly circulation of

four hundred thousand. Off Our Backs, the radical feminist
newspaper published out of Washington, DC, has a monthly
circulation of eight thousand.[20] And these figures do not
account for pass-along readership.

Consider the implications of the following example.
In 1980, the film 9 to 5 came to the movie houses and was
an instant success with women viewers. It inspired the
founding of an organization for women office workers called
"9 to 5" that now has branches in major cities all over the
United States. Yet the Rhode Island Feminist Theatre (RIFT)
first produced Paper Weight a year before 9 to 5 was ever
shown. Paper Weight has fantasy scenes similar to the ones
in 9 to 5 and focuses on similar problems faced by women
office workers. At a performance of Paper Weight in 1981,
an audience member asked the theatre group why they copied
the film.[21] RIFT explained that their own play preceded the
film by at least a year and that it was sheer coincidence that
both contained the sequence of fantasies acted out by the characters. In an interview, RIFT said:

> We tend to be a vanguard in some ways, in coming
> up with the topic before it's of major interest to
> the public. When we heard that 9 to 5 was coming
> out after we already had Paper Weight, and heard
> about the similarities, it was pretty amazing to us.[22]

What if Paper Weight had been a Broadway play before being
adapted into a film similar to 9 to 5? Now wouldn't that say
something about the potential of theatre to function as a catalyst for change in regard to women's issues? Unfortunately,
Paper Weight remains a relatively unknown drama.

Even a comparison of "live performance" media reveals a sharp difference in the number of people who attend
feminist events. A feminist theatre performance will accom-
modate between one hundred and two hundred people. A feminist concert, featuring many of the artists who record for
the Olivia label, may draw an audience of thousands.[23] When
asked about the efficacy of feminist theatre as a communication
medium, playwright Bobbi Ausubel of Caravan Theatre re-
sponded:

> Women's theatre? It's women's music that's gone
> "bazonkas" lately. In Boston a woman musician
> comes and there's five thousand people in the audi-
> ence just like that. At a festival in Michigan over
> ten thousand women [show up]. So the new women's
> music is a very conscious way of doing what I think

we set out to do in women's theatre. But music
seems to be able to address itself--I don't know
why--but whatever it is, it's popular now in a way
that theatre isn't. So you can get a mint of people
turning out for a Holly Near or Chris Williamson.
And there's a lot of rhetoric that goes on at the concerts. They're very exciting and there's a lot of
information being passed ... and a lot of rhetoric. [24]

This kind of response from a person who has done feminist
theatre work since 1965 is really astounding. Even more
astonishing is the consideration of the potential impact of a
one-shot message in the concert vs. the theatre as rhetorical
situations. The number of people who attend concerts indicates
that feminist artists will have a better chance of persuading
through song than drama. Moreover, audience members who
are receptive to what they hear at a concert can go buy the
record.
        All of this discussion, however, is not intended to
discredit feminist theatre or even to suggest that the success
of the medium is negligible. There is considerable agreement
among the artists in the feminist theatre community that it
is the quality of impact rather than quantity that makes feminist theatre not only a viable mode of communication, but
an essential one. It is the profundity of the communication
experience that makes the theatre's message so important.
The participatory nature of much of feminist theatre is a contributing factor to the impact of the message.
        In an interview with members of the Theatre of Light
and Shadow of New Haven, Connecticut, I asked what they
thought of theatre as a voice for the women's movement. The
following exchange took place in response to that question:

Nancy Kathan: Something happens when there's a play going
(director)   on on the stage and there's an audience re-
                 acting to it. There's a communication going
                 on there. That kind of theatrical moment
                 and the power of that theatrical moment is
                 very, very powerful. More powerful than
                 just sitting there reading something because
                 you're all by yourself and you're reading
                 something that's already been processed and
                 now you're putting it in; whereas in the the-
                 atrical situation there's all that back and forth
                 stuff going on.

Interviewer: Direct experience? In other words would you

> say a theatre experience would last a lot
> longer in the mind of someone than, say,
> reading a newspaper article?

June Lewin: Absolutely! Living images--there's nothing
(actress)   like them![25]

There are a number of women involved with feminist
theatre who relate the testimony of audience members as
evidence of the impact of the theatre experience. Roberta
Sklar is often quoted on the story she tells about the women
she knew who changed their lives as a result of seeing performances by It's All Right To Be Woman Theatre. Charlotte
Rea describes several instances in which the effect of a feminist performance was more than just transitory for the wom-
en in the audience.[26] Bobbi Ausubel of Caravan Theatre
tells about a woman she met on a Boston street who had
seen a performance of How to Make a Woman many years
earlier:

> I just got a letter in the mail from a woman who
> sent me an excerpt from her diary which she had
> written in 1971. She met me somewhere and came
> up to me in the street the other day and said, "I
> always wanted to thank you, etc., etc., it changed
> my life. " I always get a lot of the "it changed my
> life" stories.[27]

This illustration is significant. The message of the play that
Caravan put on stuck in the mind of this woman for eleven
years. How many other women have been affected by such
a theatrical moment?
     One of the interesting effects on an audience is the
kind of chain reaction that occurs when feminist theatre members or feminist artists witness the performances of other
feminist theatre groups. An outstanding example is the way
the group, It's All Right To Be Woman, inspired so many
other women to found their own theatre group. It's All Right
To Be Woman, formed in 1970, was one of the first feminist
theatres and it set the precedent for many of the feminist
theatres that followed in the 1970's. Roberta Sklar has cred-
ited this group, over and over again, with providing the im-
petus for the phenomenon known as women's theatre.[28] Sklar
reaffirmed this at a recent conference when she said:

> I was very fortunate to be exposed to the women of
> It's All Right To Be Woman Theatre in 1970. And

> it raised the question for me, what are the themes
> that are to be dealt with in the theatre? What are
> the vital themes for me, Roberta Sklar? It [women's
> theatre] has been a process of discovering those
> themes. 29

One founding member of It's All Right To Be Woman, Sue
Perlgut, recently said that hundreds of women had acknowledged the impact of that theatre on their lives. In fact, the
whole experience for Perlgut was so complex that she has
not been able to participate in any organized theatre activity
since It's All Right To Be Woman broke up in 1976. She
said it was, indeed, an experience that changed her own life
and something that she is "still trying to sort out. "30
    Other women attest to the internal influence of fem-
inist theatre performances. Nancy Kathan, director and actress in the Theatre of Light and Shadow, said she was active
in both college theatre and the women's movement when she
attended Wesleyan University. During a "women's weekend, "
she saw the Rhode Island Feminist Theatre perform:

> I saw RIFT in Taking It Off and a tonal monologue
> on rape by Naomi Weisstein. In seeing feminist
> theatre it was bringing together two things that I
> wanted to do, so when the Theatre of Light and
> Shadow was starting, and there was the opportunity
> for me to get involved, I couldn't wait to jump
> right in. Those experiences of my seeing feminist
> theatre had been so powerful for me they were
> still resonating inside. 31

June Lewin, also a member of the Theatre of Light and
Shadow, tells how her experience as a member of Caravan
Theatre in 1974 profoundly changed her perspective on theatre
and provided the reason she continues to participate in it.
She has worked in feminist theatre ever since her year-in-
residence with Caravan.
    This writer met Nancy Kathan and June Lewin, along
with two members of Calliope Feminist Theatre, at a performance by the Rhode Island Feminist Theatre. RIFT performed two plays that weekend, Internal Injury and Paper
Weight. 32 Apparently Internal Injury affected other feminist
artists because the following season both Calliope and Theatre
of Light and Shadow produced their own plays on the subject
of battered women. This kind of "response to a response"
is typical of feminist theatre. At any one time, a number
of plays on the same topic are being simultaneously performed

around the country by various feminist theatres.

During 1982-83, a popular subject of feminist drama was "fat as a feminist issue." The Women's Experimental Theatre in New York put on Food in the 1981-82 season as the first of a "series of plays about woman's daily unrelenting relationship to food."[33] Present Stage in Northampton, Massachusetts, has a play in repertory called Food Fright, "a show about women and food."[34] The Thesbian Feminists of Albany, New York, do a short vignette called "Carbohydrates" as part of their evennig of entertainment designed to "educate, persuade, and entertain."[35] It is interesting that these recent feminist plays deal with a woman's body and the relationship of food intake to body weight and emotional health because some of the very first feminist plays, such as RIFT's Taking It Off, deal with the very same issue. Could this be an indication of a cycle of interests that runs within the women's movement? Or are these new plays just a reaction to what other groups are currently doing?

Several generalizations can be drawn from the evidence that has been presented in this chapter. First, the content of feminist drama is radical. The issues discussed and the solutions offered in the plays are outside society's status quo. Second, there is unanimous agreement among leaders in feminist theatres that the women's movement is directly responsible for their existence and that they give their art and ideas back to the efforts of the movement.[36] Third, although the number of people that feminist theatre reaches is small when compared to other media, there is a strong indication that the theatre experience is profound and makes a great personal impact on audience members. Finally, feminist theatre groups exert a continuous influence upon each other, conditioning the attitudes of women in the groups both as artists and as participants in the women's movement.

NOTES

1. Robin Morgan, ed., Sisterhood Is Powerful (New York: Vintage Books, 1970), pp. xxviii-xxix.

2. Patti Gillespie, "Feminist Theatre: A Rhetorical Phenomenon," The Quarterly Journal of Speech, 64 (1978), p. 293.

3. Kathie Sarachild, "Consciousness-Raising: A Radi-

ical Weapon, " in Feminist Revolution, ed. Redstockings of the Women's Liberation Movement
(New York: Random House, 1975), p. 144.

4. Morgan, op. cit., p. xx.

5. Taped response by Sherilyn Brown on behalf of the
   Rhode Island Feminist Theatre to interview questions, received September 1981.

6. Some of the women mentioned were recently written about in a New York Times Magazine cover
   story. Not one of the leading participants in feminist theatre was mentioned in that article. See
   Mel Gussow, "Women Playwrights: New Voices in
   the Theater, " The New York Times Magazine,
   1 May 1983, pp. 22ff.

7. "Politics of the Ego: A Manifesto for N.Y. Radical Feminists, " in Radical Feminism, ed. Anne
   Koedt, et al. (New York: Quadrangle Books, 1973),
   p. 379.

8. For a concise explanation of the different divisions
   of feminist ideology, see Evelyn and Barry Shapiro,
   eds., The Women Say, The Men Say (New York:
   Delta, 1979), pp. xxiv-xxvi. It is especially important to note the difference between radical feminism and socialist feminism. The discussion in
   this chapter is based on the ideology of the radical
   feminists.

9. For further discussion of the pro-woman line, see
   Carol Hanisch, "The Personal Is Political, " in
   Notes from the Second Year, ed. Shulamith Firestone
   and Anne Koedt (New York: n.p., 1970), p. 77;
   and Brenda Hancock, "Affirmation by Negation in
   the Women's Liberation Movement, " The Quarterly
   Journal of Speech, 58 (1972), pp. 268-69.

10. Myrna Lamb, The Mod Donna and Scyklon Z (New
    York: Pathfinder Press, 1971), p. 157.

11. Clare Coss, Sondra Segal, and Roberta Sklar, "The
    Daughters Cycle: Electra Speaks, " Union Seminary
    Quarterly Review, 35 (1980), pp. 223-25.

12. "Politics of the Ego: A Manifesto for N.Y.; Radical Feminists, " op. cit., p. 381.

13. Betty Friedan, "Twenty Years After the Feminine Mystique," The New York Times Magazine, 27 February 1983, p. 57.

14. Program notes from The End of War, The New Cycle Theater at St. Ann's Church, Brooklyn, NY, 22 May 1982.

15. Publicity flyer received from Martha Boesing on behalf of At the Foot of the Mountain, September 1982. This quote originally appeared in a review of the play in the Minneapolis Star and Tribune, 14 May 1982.

16. Written response to author's general questionnaire received from Rose Marie Whiteley on behalf of Omaha Magic Theatre, July 1982.

17. Personal conversation with Sue Perlgut in Albany, NY, 19 March 1983.

18. Dinah Leavitt, Feminist Theatre Groups (Jefferson, NC: McFarland and Co., 1980), p. 68.

19. Information packet received from Wilma Marcus on behalf of the planning committee for the National Festival of Women's Theatre, January 1983.

20. Circulation figures for Ms. and Off Our Backs from Ulrich's International Periodicals Directory, 21st ed. (New York: R.R. Bowker Co., 1982), vol. II, p. 1787.

21. Rhode Island Feminist Theatre, Paper Weight, dir. Janet Buchwald, Educational Center for the Arts, New Haven, CT 21 November 1981.

22. Taped resonse by Sherilyn Brown on behalf of the Rhode Island Feminist Theatre to interview questions, received September 1981.

23. See Pamela Brandt, "The New Woman Sound Hits the Charts, " Ms., September 1980, pp. 66-67, 88, 97; and "Holly Near: Staying Out of the Closet and Off the Charts, " People, 13 July 1981, pp. 103-04.

24. Personal interview with Bobbi Ausubel in New Haven, CT, 31 March 1982.

25. Personal interview with members of the Theatre of Light and Shadow in New Haven, CT, 1 April 1982.

26. Charlotte Rea, "Women for Women," The Drama Review, 18 (December 1974), pp. 81-83. The Sklar story was originally quoted by Rea in this article, and has since been quoted again in several articles on feminist theatre by other authors.

27. Personal interview with Bobbi Ausubel in New Haven, CT, 31 March 1982.

28. See Rea, op. cit., p. 81 and Cornelia Brunner, "Roberta Sklar: Toward Creating a Women's Theatre," The Drama Review, 24 (June 1980), p. 35.

29. Roberta Sklar, "The New Women's Theatre" panel discussion, Women in Theatre Conference, New Haven, CT, 31 March 1982.

30. Personal conversation with Sue Perlgut in Albany, NY, 19 March 1983.

31. Personal interview with Nancy Kathan and other members of the Theatre of Light and Shadow in New Haven, CT, 1 April 1982.

32. See note 20. Internal Injury was performed on 20 November 1981 at the same location.

33. Program received from Sondra Segal on behalf of the Women's Experimental Theatre, March 1982. Foodtalk, the second play in the series, was produced at Women's Interart Theatre in July 1982.

34. Publicity material from Present Stage Theatre obtained in March 1983.

35. Program note from a Thesbian Feminist performance, Page Hall, SUNY-Albany, 19 March 1983. The Thesbian Feminists performed as part of a conference entitled Critical Stages: Women In American Theatre, sponsored by the Women's Studies Program at SUNYA.

36. Every theatre group that provided data for this
     study acknowledged the women's movement as the
     direct inspiration for their theatre, and all said
     they felt they were a part of the women's movement
     through their contributions as feminist theatre art-
     ists.

Chapter Eight
CONCLUSION

      This study has made a comprehensive attempt to determine the rhetorical nature of feminist theatre. The premises were established that feminist theatre is a form of persuasive communication and that the messages which emerge from the drama are directly linked to the radical ideology of the women's movement.

      The framework for discussion in the previous chapters was based on a model that depicted feminist theatre as a multi-locational rhetorical process. The word "process" is a key to the way in which feminist theatre groups function as communicators. From the earliest groups--who fashioned drama out of experiences revealed in consciousness-raising sessions--to the most recent groups--who conduct sophisticated research when constructing a drama--there is constant in-group communication that leads to the presentation of a message to an audience. No two groups work in exactly the same way, even though the outcomes have striking similarities. The women's movement has always functioned in a fragmented form, in the sense that groups of people are simultaneously creating and exchanging ideas in locales that may be many miles apart. The feminist theatre groups, which do function as an element of the women's movement, are no different. The twenty plays examined in this study are thought to be representative of the general ideas that are circulating among the one hundred plus theatre groups that currently exist in the United States.

      A question was raised in Chapter Six as to whether feminist theatres aim their messages at people outside the women's movement, or whether the drama is for the benefit of other "sisters." The evidence presented makes a strong case for the latter. Using audience demographics, testimony from theatre groups, and observations of performances, the premise was developed that feminist theatre functions for the benefit of other feminists, and that the rhetorical strategies in the drama serve to strengthen the feminist beliefs of both audience members and the members of the theatre group. The strengthening process is aided by the audience participation that often

accompanies performance as well as by the actual enactment
of the drama by the actors.

The effects of enactment need further investigation.
This study has focused primarily on the words that express
the thoughts of the playwrights. The method of analysis relied strictly on Aristotle's Rhetoric, and excluded the effect
that nonverbal communication can exert in a persuasive appeal.
Action as persuasion is more properly the domain of the
Poetics, and was purposely left out of consideration. A recent article by Charles Kauffman makes a strong suggestion
that enactment is an integral part of argument in didactic
drama. He says:

> Aristotle seems to distinguish two forms of argu-
> ment within poetic discourse: a form which pro-
> ceeds through speech, producing proofs for its con-
> clusions, and a second form which proceeds through
> enactment, "without explicit argument." Argument
> seems to be more than a verbal phenomenon; the
> Poetics seems to extend the range of argument to
> include dramatic enactment.[1]

Perhaps further investigation of feminist drama could include
principles from both the Poetics and the Rhetoric for a more
thorough understanding of the way in which drama and discourse are combined for persuasive effect.

The analysis of plays in this study was not designed
to delineate a feminist dramatic aesthetic. Indeed, an aesthetic based on Aristotelian standards would more than likely
be immediately rejected by feminists! Janet Brown's aesthetic based on the dramatistic pentad of Kenneth Burke has
already been dismissed as a "coolly analytical and patriarchal
formalistic approach to feminist drama criticism."[2] The
theatre scholars who are currently working toward establishing
aesthetic standards of criticism lean toward commonalities of
theme, character types, language, and structural devices that
are distinctly feminist, but the plays they examine for such
principles are not ones authored by feminist theatre groups.[3]

An Aristotelian approach has some value, however,
if we want to analyze feminist drama as rhetoric instead of
theatre. The rhetorical features of feminist writing and
speaking outlined by Karlyn Campbell were evident in the
drama examined in this study.[4] An aesthetic based on rhetorical principles may, indeed, provide insight into the structure and function of feminist drama, and does not appear
entirely incompatible with other approaches.

The discussion of feminist drama as belief-bolstering

persuasion needs further validation. This study makes strong
suggestions that the audience and actors share similar political beliefs, but securing actual audience response to confirm this notion is limited. It is almost an understatement
to say that passing out audience response questionnaires at
a performance is logistically difficult. Furthermore, requests
to do this are often rejected by the theatre group as an in-
trusion on a performance which they want to control. Some
theatre groups do survey their own audiences. [5] If researchers
could have access to those results, perhaps further confirmation of the belief-bolstering idea could be established.

The theory of belief-bolstering stemmed from the feeling that women had moved into a psychological awareness
beyond the consciousness-raising (CR) stage. However, the
analysis of plays indicates that the features of CR are em-
bedded in much of the drama. A recent performance by a
theatre group that utilized material which obviously came
right out of their own "bitch sessions" [6] further underscores
this point. Paradoxically, the audience at that performance
did not respond as naive truth-seekers who were having their
consciousness raised for the first time. They heartily clapped
and cheered throughout the performance, which indicated
their prior agreement with the ideas expressed in the drama.
When one considers that many theatre groups still begin
every rehearsal or business meeting with a CR session, then
a conclusion can be drawn about the psychological pattern
that occurs in feminist theatre as a communication process.
Consciousness-raising is an ongoing psychological habit of
any feminist. Ideas are brought from the subconscious to
a level of overt awareness. Belief-bolstering occurs when
those ideas are articulated over and over again. Feminist
drama, which serves as a means of articulating those ideas,
is imbued with CR techniques as rhetorical strategies. The
audience responds to those strategies by reenacting a process
(and its resultant ideas) that they have already engaged in.
The pattern recurs again and again: explore an idea, articulate the idea, reaffirm the idea. Feminist theatre as a
rhetorical phenomenon allows the pattern to repeat itself in
an effort to "overcome an active opposition [men and anti-
feminists] and, simultaneously, contribute to the attractive-
ness and credibility of [feminist] ideas. "[7]

This brings us to the question of time. When the
Equal Rights Amendment was defeated, there was speculation
from the opposition that the women's movement was also near
death. A recent New York Times article by a feminist in
her thirties revealed that the new generation of women is
decidedly conservative and does not support the women's

movement the way women supported it ten years ago.[8] If
feminism is on the way out, then the question is, will feminist theatre go out with it?

The phenomenon may be small but many women active
in theatre arts believe that feminist theatre is firmly established.
Feminist theatre activity is ongoing. The National Festival
of Women's Theatre ran for a week in May 1983 and featured
performances exclusively by feminist theatre groups. Also
in 1983, SUNY at Albany held a weekend conference on women
in theatre. The Performance Studies Department of New York
University just recently published the first issue of a new
journal of feminist theory entitled Women and Performance.
At the 1983 American Theatre Association Convention, the
Women's Program Preconvention featured performances by
several leading and new groups in feminist theatre, including
At the Foot of the Mountain, Present Stage, and The Split
Britches Theater Company. The performances by the feminist groups were so well received that the Women's Program
planned a similar preconvention for the summer of 1984.
Finally, Karen Malpede's new book, entitled Women in Theatre: Compassion and Hope, profiles some of the women who
are currently active in feminist theatre. These facts suggest that as long as there are women who feel they must
articulate their ideas of feminism, feminist theatre groups
will continue to exist. Historically, the stage has served
as a rhetorical platform, and there is no reason to believe
that feminists will abandon it now.

NOTES

1.   Charles Kauffman, "Poetic As Argument," The
     Quarterly Journal of Speech, 67 (1981), p. 411.

2.   Beverly Byers Pevitts, Feminist Thematic Trends
     in Plays written by Women for the American
     Theatre: 1970-1979, Diss. Southern Illinois Univ.
     1980 (Ann Arbor: University Microfilms, 1982),
     p. 31.

3.   The plays that are being studied come from women
     playwrights who seek financial success and critical
     acclaim from their work. Pevitts' study includes
     drama by these women. (See note above.) Janet
     Brown also selected these kinds of plays for her

study of feminist drama. See note 46 in Chapter
Two. The most recent profile of mainstream
feminist writers is Mel Gussow's article, "Women
Playwrights: New Voices in the Theater," The
New York Times Magazine, 1 May 1983, pp. 22ff.

4. See Chapter Five, p. 91.

5. For example, At the Foot of the Mountain and
Theatre of Light and Shadow have made attempts
to gather from their audiences demographics and
reactions to plays presented. ATFM offered the
results of a 1982 survey, but the data were not
appropriate responses to the questions asked. This
is to be expected, but if a larger number of surveys were examined, some generalizations might
be drawn concerning political beliefs of feminist
theatre audiences.

6. "Bitch session" is the term used by Kathie Sarachild in her article, "A Program for Feminist
'Consciousness-Raising,'" in Notes from the Second Year, ed. Shulamith Firestone and Anne Koedt
(New York: n.p., 1970), p. 79.

7. Edwin Black, Rhetorical Criticism (New York:
Macmillan, 1965), p. 150. This author has sub-
stituted the word "feminist" for "the rhetor's" in
this quotation.

8. Susan Bolotin, "Voices from the Post-Feminist
Generation," The New York Times Magazine, 17
October 1982, pp. 29ff.

BIBLIOGRAPHY

Books

Barlow, Judith, ed. Plays by American Women: The Early Years.
New York: Avon Books, 1981.

Bentley, Eric. The Theatre of Commitment. New York: Atheneum,
1967.

Black, Edwin. Rhetorical Criticism: A Study in Method. New York:
Macmillan, 1965.

Booth, Michael R. English Melodrama. London: Herbert Jenkins,
1965.

Brecht, Bertold. "Theatre for Pleasure or Theatre for Instruction."
In Brecht on Theatre. Trans. John Willett. New York: Hill
and Wang, 1964.

Brockett, Oscar G., and Robert R. Findlay. Century of Innovation:
A History of European and American Theatre and Drama Since
1870. Englewood Cliffs, NJ: Prentice-Hall, 1973.

Brown, Janet. Feminist Drama: Definition and Critical Analysis.
Metuchen, NJ: Scarecrow Press, 1979.

Butcher, S.H., trans. Aristotle's Poetics. Introd. Francis Fergusson.
New York: Hill and Wang, 1961.

Chinoy, Helen Kirch, and Linda Walsh Jenkins, eds. Women in
American Theatre. New York: Crown Publishers, 1981.

Cooper, Lane, trans. The Rhetoric of Aristotle. Englewood Cliffs,
NJ: Prentice-Hall, 1932.

Croyden, Margaret. Lunatics, Lovers and Poets: The Contemporary
Experimental Theatre. New York: McGraw-Hill, 1974.

de Beauvoir, Simone. The Second Sex. Trans. H.M. Parshley.
New York: Vintage Books, 1952.

Evans, Sara. Personal Politics: The Roots of Women's Liberation
in the Civil Rights Movement and the New Left. New York:
Alfred Knopf, 1979.

Festinger, Leon. A Theory of Cognitive Dissonance. Evanston, IL: Row, Peterson, 1957.

Friday, Nancy. My Mother/My Self. New York: Dell Books, 1977.

Friedan, Betty. The Feminine Mystique. New York: Dell Books, 1963.

_____. The Second Stage. New York: Summit Books, 1981.

Heilman, Robert Bechtold. Tragedy and Melodrama: Versions of Experience. Seattle: Univ. of Washington Press, 1968.

Himelstein, Morgan. Drama Was a Weapon: The Left-Wing Theatre in New York, 1929-1941. New Brunswick, NJ: Rutgers Univ. Press, 1963.

Koedt, Anne, Ellen Levine, and Anita Rapone, eds. Radical Feminism. New York: Quandrangle Books, 1973.

Leavitt, Dinah Luise. Feminist Theatre Groups. Jefferson, NC: McFarland and Co., 1980.

McGuigan, Dorothy G., ed. Women's Lives: New Theory, Research, and Policy. Ann Arbor: Univ. of Michigan Press, 1980.

Malpede, Karen, ed. Women in Theatre: Compassion & Hope. New York: Drama Book Publishers, 1983.

Martin, Wendy, ed. The American Sisterhood. New York: Harper and Row, 1972.

Millett, Kate. Sexual Politics. Garden City, NY: Doubleday, 1970.

Moore, Donna, ed. Battered Women. Beverly Hills: Sage Publications, 1979.

Morgan, Robin. The Anatomy of Freedom: Feminism, Physics, and Global Politics. Garden City, NY: Anchor Books, 1982.

_____, ed. Sisterhood Is Powerful: An Anthology of Writings from The Women's Liberation Movement. New York: Vintage Books, 1970.

Nannes, Caspar. Politics in the American Drama. Washington, DC: The Catholic Univ. of America Press, 1960.

Olsen, Tillie. Tell Me a Riddle. London: Faber and Faber, 1964.

Pevitts, Beverley Byers. Feminist Thematic Trends in Plays Written by Women for the American Theatre; 1970-1979. Diss. Southern Illinois Univ. 1980. Ann Arbor: Univ. Microfilms International, 1982.

Rokeach, Milton. Beliefs, Attitudes, and Values. San Francisco:
    Jossey-Bass, 1973.

Sainer, Arthur. The Radical Theatre Notebook. New York: Avon
    Books, 1975.

Shapiro, Evelyn, and Barry Shapiro, eds. The Women Say, The
    Men Say. New York: Delta, 1979.

Shaw, Bernard. Plays Unpleasant. London: Penguin Books, 1946.

Smiley, Sam. The Drama of Attack: Didactic Plays of the American
    Depression. Columbia: Univ. of Missouri Press, 1972.

                            Articles

Billman, Carol. "Women and the Family in American Drama."
    The Arizona Quarterly, 36 (1980), pp. 35-48.

Black, Edwin. "The Second Persona." The Quarterly Journal of
    Speech, 56 (1970), pp. 109-19.

Bolotin, Susan. "Voices from the Post-Feminist Generation."
    The New York Times Magazine. 17 October 1982, pp. 29ff.

Bosworth, Patricia. "The Arts: Risk Theater." Working Woman,
    August 1982, pp. 92, 94-95.

Brandt, Pamela. "The New Woman Sound Hits the Charts." Ms.,
    September 1980, pp. 66ff.

Brunner, Cornelia. "Roberta Sklar: Toward Creating a Women's
    Theatre." The Drama Review, 24, No. 2 (1980), pp. 23-40.

Campbell, Karlyn Kohrs. "The Rhetoric of Women's Liberation:
    An Oxymoron." The Quarterly Journal of Speech, 59 (1973),
    pp. 74-86.

Cohn, Ruby. "Joan Holden and the San Francisco Mime Troupe."
    The Drama Review, 24, No. 2 (1980), pp. 41-50.

Coss, Clare, Sondra Segal, and Roberta Sklar. "The Daughters
    Cycle: Electra Speaks." Union Seminary Quarterly Review,
    35, Nos. 3 and 4 (1980), pp. 223-253.

Curb, Rosemary. "Catalog of Feminist Theatre--Part 2." Chrysalis,
    No. 10 (1979), pp. 63-75.

_____. "Mounting Anger into Power: Alienation and Channeled
    Anger in Women's Theater." Unpublished Manuscript, 1982.

_____, Phyllis Mael, and Beverley Byers Pevitts. "Catalog of
Feminist Theatre--Part 1. "Chrysalis, No. 10 (1979), pp. 51-62.

Dell'Olio, Anselma. "The Founding of the New Feminist Theater."
In Notes from the Second Year: Women's Liberation, Major
Writings of the Radical Feminists. Eds. Shulamith Firestone
and Anne Koedt. New York: n.p., 1970, pp. 101-02.

Dullea, Georgia. "Dreams Are What a Feminist Group's Plays Are
Made Of." New York Times, 21 December 1972, Sec. 1, p.
42, cols. 1-6.

Footlick, Jerrold, and Elaine Sciolino. "Wives Who Batter Back."
Newsweek, 30 January 1978, p. 54.

Friedan, Betty. "Feminism's Next Step." New York Times Magazine, 5 July 1981, pp. 12ff.

_____. "Twenty Years After the Feminine Mystique." New York
Times Magazine, 27 February 1983, pp. 34ff.

Gillespie, Patti P. "Feminist Theatre: A Rhetorical Phenomenon."
The Quarterly Journal of Speech, 64 (1978), pp. 284-94.

_____. "Feminist Theatres of the 1970's." Theatre News, 10
No. 2 (1977), pp. 5, 19.

_____. "A Listing of Feminist Theaters." Theatre News, 10,
No. 2 (1977), pp. 22-24.

Gussow, Mel. "New Group to Offer Plays by Women." The New
York Times, 22 February 1972, Sec. 1, p. 44, cols. 1-4.

_____. "Stage: Feminist Musical." The New York Times, 19
June 1973, Sec. 1, p. 30, cols. 3-4.

_____. "Theater: Women's Work." The New York Times, 30
March 1976, Sec. 1, p. 39, cols. 2-3.

_____. "Women Playwrights: New Voices in the Theater," The
New York Times Magazine, 1 May 1983, pp. 22-27, 30, 33,
34, 36, 38, 40.

Hancock, Brenda Robinson. "Affirmation by Negation in the Women's
Liberation Movement." The Quarterly Journal of Speech, 58
(1972), pp. 264-71.

Hanisch, Carol. "The Personal Is Political." In Notes from the
Second Year: Women's Liberation, Major Writings of the
Radical Feminists. Eds. Shulamith Firestone and Anne Koedt.
New York: n.p., 1970, pp. 76-78.

"Holly Near: Staying Out of the Closet and Off the Charts." People,
13 July 1981, pp. 103-04.

Kauffman, Charles. "Poetic As Argument." The Quarterly Journal
    of Speech, 67 (1981), pp. 407-15.

Killian, Linda. "Feminist Theatre." Feminist Art Journal, No. 3
    (1974), pp. 23-24.

Kirby, Michael. "On Political Theatre." The Drama Review, 19,
    No. 2 (1975), pp. 129-35.

Lamb, Margaret. "Feminist Criticism." The Drama Review, 18,
    No. 3 (1974), pp. 46-50.

McGuire, William J. "Inducing Resistance to Persuasion: Some
    Contemporary Approaches." In Advances in Experimental
    Social Psychology. Vol. I. Ed. Leonard Berkowitz. New
    York: Academic Press, 1964, pp. 191-229.

_____. "The Nature of Attitudes and Attitude Change." In The
    Handbook of Social Psychology. Eds. G. Lindsey and E.
    Aronson. Reading, Mass.: Addison-Wesley, 1969, pp. 136-314.

_____. "Resistance to Persuasion Conferred by Active and Pas-
    sive Prior Refutation of the Same and Alternative Counterargu-
    ments." Journal of Abnormal and Social Psychology, 63 (1961),
    pp. 326-32.

Moore, Honor. "Can You Talk About Your Mother Without Crying?"
    Ms., November 1977, pp. 29-30.

Morgan, Robin. "Art and Feminism: A One-Act Whimsical Amuse-
    ment on All That Matters." Chrysalis, No. 2 (1977), pp.
    69-87.

"Ms. Gazette News." Ms., December 1977, pp. 89-90.

Perinciolo, Lillian. "Feminist Theatre: They're Playing in Peoria."
    Ms., October 1975, pp. 101-04.

Radicalesbians. "The Woman-Identified Woman." In Out of the
    Closets: Voices of Gay Liberation. Eds. Karla Jay and Allen
    Young. New York: Douglas Book Corp., 1972.

Rea, Charlotte. "The New York Feminist Theatre Troupe." The
    Drama Review, 18, no. 3 (1974), pp. 132-33.

_____. "Women for Women." The Drama Review, 18, No.
    4 (1974), pp. 77-87.

_____. "Women's Theatre Groups." The Drama Review, 16,
    No. 2 (1972), pp. 79-89.

Regelson, Rosalyn. "Is Motherhood Holy? Not Any More." New
    York Times, 18 May 1969, Sec. 2, p. 1.

142   FEMINIST THEATRE

Sarachild, Kathie. "Consciousness-Raising: A Radical Weapon."
In Feminist Revolution (An Abridged Edition with Additional
Writings). Eds. Redstockings of the Women's Liberation
Movement. New York: Random House, 1975, pp. 144-50.

_____. "A Program For Feminist 'Consciousness Raising.'" In
Notes From the Second Year: Women's Liberation, Major
Writings of the Radical Feminists. Eds. Shulamith Firestone
and Anne Koedt. New York: n.p., 1970, pp. 78-80.

Sisley, Emily L. "Notes on Lesbian Theatre." The Drama Review,
25, no. 1 (1981), pp. 47-56.

Smiley, Sam. "Rhetorical Principles in Didactic Drama." The
Quarterly Journal of Speech, 57 (1971), pp. 147-52.

Taylor, Karen Malpede. "It's All Right To Be Woman Theatre."
In People's Theatre In Amerika. New York: Drama Book
Publishers, 1972, pp. 325-28.

Plays

Published

Chambers, Jane. A Late Snow. In Gay Plays: The First Collection.
Ed. William Hoffman. New York: Avon Books, 1979.

France, Rachel, ed. A Century of Plays by American Women.
New York: Richard Rosen Press, 1979.

Holden, Joan. The Independent Female (Or, A Man Has His Pride).
In Notes from the Third Year: Women's Liberation. Eds.
Anne Koedt and Shulamith Firestone. New York: n.p., 1971,
pp. 120-31.

Lamb, Myrna. The Mod Donna and Scyklon Z. New York: Pathfinder Press, 1971.

LaTempa, Susan, ed. New Plays by Women. Berkeley: Shame-
less Hussy Press, 1979.

Moore, Honor. The New Women's Theatre. New York: Vintage
Books, 1977.

Rhode Island Feminist Theatre. The Johnnie Show. Providence:
n.p., 1974.

_____. Persephones Return. Providence: n.p., 1975.

_____. Taking It Off. Providence: Hellcoal Press, 1973.

Shange, Ntozake. for colored girls who have considered suicide/ when the rainbow is enuf. New York: Bantam Books, 1980.

Sullivan, Victoria, and James Hatch, eds. Plays By and About Women. New York: Vintage Books, 1974.

Terry, Megan. American King's English for Queens. Omaha: Omaha Magic Theatre Press, 1978.

_____. Babes in the Bighouse. Omaha: Omaha Magic Theatre Press, 1974.

_____. Keep Tightly Closed in a Cool, Dry Place. In Four Plays. New York: Touchstone, 1966.

Wasserstein, Wendy. Uncommon Women and Others. New York: Avon Books, 1978.

Unpublished

Ausubel, Bobbi. Focus On Me! Boston, 1974.

_____. How to Make a Woman. Boston, 1970.

_____. Tell Me a Riddle. Boston, 1977.

Boesing, Martha. Love Song for an Amazon. Minneapolis, 1976.

_____. River Journal. Minneapolis, 1975.

_____. The Web. Minneapolis, 1981.

Calliope Feminist Theatre. Make Up by Mother Nature. Hartford, 1982.

Malpede, Karen. The End of War. New York, 1977. Revised 1982.

Rhode Island Feminist Theatre. Internal Injury. Providence, 1979.

_____. Paper Weight. Providence, 1979.

Unpublished Primary Sources

Abrams, Rosalie Gresser. Copies of correspondence to Ms., publicity flyers on behalf of Orange County Feminist Theatre, 4 October 1981.

Ausubel, Bobbi. Newspaper articles on behalf of Caravan Theatre, 31 March 1982.

Boesing, Martha. Results of audience poll, publicity flyers, play
    descriptions on behalf of At the Foot of the Mountain, September
    1982.

Brown, Sherilyn. Extensive taped responses on behalf of Rhode Island
    Feminist Theatre to written interview questions, September 1981.

Dailey, Sharon. Questionnaire responses, program on behalf of the
    Indiana State University Interpretation Ensemble, 15 March 1982.

Forman, Joanne. Letter to author. 28 January 1982.

Hopkins, Rosemary. Questionnaire responses, publicity flyer on
    behalf of Eccentric Circles Theatre, 11 February 1982.

Leavitt, Dinah. Questionnaire responses on behalf of Boulder Fem-
    inist Theatre Collective, 19 February 1982.

Lewin, June. Publicity brochure, theatre description, conference
    materials on behalf of Theatre of Light and Shadow, December
    1981.

Marcus, Wilma. Newsletter, policy statement, festival description
    on behalf of The National Festival of Women's Theatre, 15
    January 1983.

Mosier, Teri. Newspaper articles, touring information. audience
    responses, publicity flyers on behalf of At the Foot of the
    Mountain, 8 September 1981.

"Pro-Femina Theatre." Horizons. National Public Radio. 3 Feb-
    ruary 1981.

Rakofsky, Karen. Letter to author. 6 October 1981.

Rhode Island Feminist Theatre. Publicity brochures, production
    history, touring information, newspaper articles, job descrip-
    tions, September 1981.

Segal, Sondra. Questionnaire responses, programs, article reprint,
    audience responses on behalf of Women's Experimental Theatre,
    12 March 1982.

Whiteley, Rose Marie. Questionnaire responses, newspaper arti-
    cles, theatre resume, play descriptions on behalf of Omaha
    Magic Theatre, July 1982.

Wood, Sharon. Questionnaire responses, program, newspaper arti-
    cles, publicity flyers, play excerpts on behalf of Calliope Fem-
    inist Theatre, 21 December 1981.

Interviews

Ausubel, Bobbi, and June Lewin. Personal interview. 31 March
    1982.

Boesing, Martha. Telephone interview. 5 September 1982.

Chast, Susan, Sarah Ives, Nancy Kathan, and June Lewin. Personal
    interview. 1 April 1982.

Kearns, Martha. Personal interview. 1 March 1982.

Perlgut, Susan. Personal conversation. 19 March 1983.

Performances

Buchwald, Janet, dir. Internal Injury. The Rhode Island Feminist
    Theatre. Eagen Auditorium, University of Scranton, Scranton,
    Pa. 21 March 1982.

_____. Paper Weight. The Rhode Island Feminist Theatre. Ed-
    ucational Center for the Arts, New Haven. 21 November 1981.

Caged. It's All Right To Be Woman Theatre. Videotape, 1976.

Chast, Susan, dir. Scene from Eleanor of Aquitaine. By Ruth Wolff.
    With This River of Women Theatre Company. Page Hall, State
    University of New York, Albany. 19 March 1983.

_____. Scene from Uncommon Women and Others. By Wendy
    Wasserstein. With Theatre of Light and Shadow. Bree Audi-
    torium, Albertus Magnus College, New Haven. 31 March 1982.

Coss, Clare, Sondra Segal, and Roberta Sklar. Electra Speaks.
    Scene by Sondra Segal. Bree Auditorium, Albertus Magnus
    College, New Haven. 31 March 1982.

Cummings, Brenda, dir. Scene from Locked Out of the World. By
    Andrea Hairston. With Myra Taylor and Nancy Kathan. Bree
    Auditorium, Albertus Magnus College, New Haven. 31 March
    1982.

Kearns, Martha. King Christina. Staged Reading. Wilma Theater,
    Philadelphia. 27 May 1982.

Lewin, June, dir. Scene from Crazyhead. By Bobbi Ausubel. With
    Rachelle Mishal. Bree Auditorium, Albertus Magnus College,
    New Haven. 31 March 1982.

Linn, Hildy, dir. Scene from The Chinese Restaurant Syndrome.
   By Corrine Jacker. With This River of Women Theatre Com-
   pany. Page Hall, State University of New York, Albany. 19
   March 1983.

Lyons, Andi, dir. The Doilie Sisters. By Constance Valis and
   Sarah Safford. Page Hall, State University of New York,
   Albany. 18 March 1983.

Mischief Mime. Untitled performance. With Barbara Anger and Anne
   Rhodes. Page Hall, State University of New York, Albany.
   19 March 1983.

Shevey, Betsy, dir. The End of War. By Karen Malpede. The
   New Cycle Theater. St. Ann's Church, Brooklyn. 22 May
   1982.

The Thesbian Feminists. Untitled performance. Page Hall, State
   University of New York, Albany. 19 March 1983.

Van Dyke, Elizabeth. Love to All, Lorriane. Page Hall, State
   University of New York, Albany. 18 March 1983.

Wasserstein, Wendy. Uncommon Women and Others. Tommy's
   Deep South Music Hall, Tallahassee, Fla. 25 July 1981.

Conferences

Critical Stages: Women in American Theater. Conference sponsored
   by the Women's Studies Program, State University of New York
   at Albany, 18-20 March 1983.

"The New Women's Theatre." Program in the Women in Theatre
   Conference. Sponsored by the Theatre of Light and Shadow
   and Albertus Magnus College, New Haven, 31 March 1982.

INDEX

147